# TEACHER'S PET PUBLICATIONS

LITPLAN TEACHER PACK
for
My Ántonia
based on the book by
Willa Cather

Written by
Mary B. Collins

© 1996 Teacher's Pet Publications
All Rights Reserved

This **LitPlan** for Willa Cather's
My Antonia
has been brought to you by Teacher's Pet Publications, Inc.

Copyright Teacher's Pet Publications 1996
11504 Hammock Point
Berlin MD 21811

Only the student materials in this unit plan (such as worksheets, study questions, and tests) may be reproduced multiple times for use in the purchaser's classroom.

For any additional copyright questions,
contact Teacher's Pet Publications.

www.tpet.com

TABLE OF CONTENTS - *My Antonia*

Introduction	5
Unit Objectives	8
Reading Assignment Sheet	9
Unit Outline	10
Study Questions (Short Answer)	13
Quiz/Study Questions (Multiple Choice)	27
Pre-reading Vocabulary Worksheets	53
Introductory Lesson (Lesson One)	79
Nonfiction Assignment Sheet	81
Oral Reading Evaluation Form	82
Writing Assignment 1	85
Writing Assignment 2	89
Writing Assignment 3	92
Writing Evaluation Form	93
Vocabulary Review Activities	96
Extra Writing Assignments/Discussion ?s	94
Unit Review Activities	101
Unit Tests	105
Unit Resource Materials	135
Vocabulary Resource Materials	149

A FEW NOTES ABOUT THE AUTHOR
WILLA CATHER

CATHER, Willa (1873-1947). In such classic American novels as 'O Pioneers!' Willa Cather wrote of people she had known as a girl in Nebraska. Her friends were both native Americans and European immigrants and their children. She showed how these pioneers were able to adapt themselves to the rugged prairie life in the western area of America. For her depictions of this valiant spirit, Willa Cather won wide acclaim as a novelist.

Willa Cather was born on Dec. 7, 1873, in Winchester, Va. Her family had been Virginians for four generations. When Willa was 9 years old her father bought a ranch that was located near Red Cloud, Neb. The child was excited by the change from a settled, eastern community to a semi-frontier area where she was free to roam outdoors. Often she would ride her pony to a neighbor's farm and listen to old immigrant women tell stories of their childhood experiences and adventures in Sweden or Bohemia.

There were no schools near the ranch, so she studied at home. A neighbor taught her Latin, and Willa read English classics aloud to her grandmother. When Willa was in her teens the family moved into the village. She attended Red Cloud High School and the University of Nebraska. After graduation in 1895 she worked on a Pittsburgh newspaper for six years, then taught high school for a time. On vacations she traveled to Europe and the American Southwest.

Meanwhile, she contributed stories to McClure's Magazine. She also accepted a post on the magazine, and in 1908 she became its managing editor. But editing left her little time for creative writing, and in 1912 she resigned to devote full time to writing her own stories.

Her first novel was unsuccessful, but when she turned to frontier themes she won a wide audience. 'O Pioneers!', published in 1913, was followed by 'Song of the Lark' (1915) and 'My Antonia' (1918). 'One of Ours', which won the Pulitzer prize in 1923, and 'A Lost Lady' (1923) mourned the passing of the pioneer spirit in the Middle West. Also popular were 'Death Comes for the Archbishop' (1927), a study of Roman Catholic missionaries in New Mexico, and 'Shadows on the Rock' (1931), a story of early Quebec. She described her clean, meticulous writing style as "démeuble" (unfurnished).

Cather never married. She lived quietly in New York City or traveled in Europe, avoiding public appearances whenever possible. She remained loyal to childhood friends and visited them often. She died in New York City on April 24, 1947.

---- Courtesy of Compton's Learning Company

INTRODUCTION

This unit has been designed to develop students' reading, writing, thinking, and language skills through exercises and activities related to *My Antonia* by Willa Cather. It includes nineteen lessons, supported by extra resource materials.

The **introductory lesson** introduces students to the idea of immigration (since many of the characters in the novel are immigrants). Following the introductory activity, students are given a transition to explain how the activity relates to the book they are about to read. Following the transition, students are given the materials they will be using during the unit. At the end of the lesson, students begin the pre-reading work for the first reading assignment.

The **reading assignments** are approximately thirty pages each; some are a little shorter while others are a little longer. Students have approximately 15 minutes of pre-reading work to do prior to each reading assignment. This pre-reading work involves reviewing the study questions for the assignment and doing some vocabulary work for 8 to 10 vocabulary words they will encounter in their reading.

The **study guide questions** are fact-based questions; students can find the answers to these questions right in the text. These questions come in two formats: short answer or multiple choice. The best use of these materials is probably to use the short answer version of the questions as study guides for students (since answers will be more complete), and to use the multiple choice version for occasional quizzes. If your school has the appropriate machinery, it might be a good idea to make transparencies of your answer keys for the overhead projector.

The **vocabulary work** is intended to enrich students' vocabularies as well as to aid in the students' understanding of the book. Prior to each reading assignment, students will complete a two-part worksheet for approximately 8 to 10 vocabulary words in the upcoming reading assignment. Part I focuses on students' use of general knowledge and contextual clues by giving the sentence in which the word appears in the text. Students are then to write down what they think the words mean based on the words' usage. Part II nails down the definitions of the words by giving students dictionary definitions of the words and having students match the words to the correct definitions based on the words' contextual usage. Students should then have an understanding of the words when they meet them in the text.

After each reading assignment, students will go back and formulate answers for the study guide questions. Discussion of these questions serves as a **review** of the most important events and ideas presented in the reading assignments.

After students complete reading the work, there is a **vocabulary review** lesson which pulls together all of the fragmented vocabulary lists for the reading assignments and gives students a review of all of the words they have studied.

A lesson is devoted to the **extra discussion questions/writing assignments**. These questions focus on interpretation, critical analysis and personal response, employing a variety of thinking skills and adding to the students' understanding of the novel.

There is a **group activity** in which students work in small groups to discuss symbolism and characterization in the novel.

The group activity is followed by a **reports and discussion** session in which the groups share their ideas about the themes with the entire class; thus, the entire class is exposed to information about all of the themes and the entire class can discuss each theme based on the nucleus of information brought forth by each of the groups.

There are three **writing assignments** in this unit, each with the purpose of informing, persuading, or having students express personal opinions. The first assignment is to express personal opinions: students give their opinions as to whether the United States should continue with an open door policy towards immigrants or should impose some kind of restrictions on the number of immigrants the country will accept. The second assignment is to inform: students write a composition in preparation for the oral presentations they will make about the pioneers they have researched. The third assignment is to persuade: students pretend to be pioneers who have moved west and are writing back east to a cousin, persuading the cousin to come west, too.

In addition, there is a **nonfiction reading assignment**. Students are required to read a piece of nonfiction related in some way to *My Antonia*. After reading their nonfiction pieces, students will fill out a worksheet on which they answer questions regarding facts, interpretation, criticism, and personal opinions. During one class period, students make **oral presentations** about the nonfiction pieces they have read. This not only exposes all students to a wealth of information, it also gives students the opportunity to practice **public speaking**.

The **review lesson** pulls together all of the aspects of the unit. The teacher is given four or five choices of activities or games to use which all serve the same basic function of reviewing all of the information presented in the unit.

The **unit test** comes in two formats: multiple choice or short answer. As a convenience, two different tests for each format have been included. There is also an advanced short answer test for students who need more of a challenge.

There are additional **support materials** included with this unit. The **resource sections** include suggestions for an in-class library, crossword and word search puzzles related to the novel, and extra vocabulary worksheets. There is a list of **bulletin board ideas** which gives the teacher suggestions for bulletin boards to go along with this unit. In addition, there is a list of **extra class activities** the teacher could choose from to enhance the unit or as a substitution for an exercise the teacher might feel is inappropriate for his/her class. **Answer keys** are located directly after the **reproducible student materials** throughout the unit. The student materials may be reproduced for use in the teacher's classroom without infringement of copyrights. No other portion of this unit may be reproduced without the written consent of Teacher's Pet Publications, Inc.

UNIT OBJECTIVES - *My Antonia*

1. Students will follow the main characters as they progress from childhood to maturity, studying the Coming of Age theme.

2. Students will demonstrate their understanding of the text on four levels: factual, interpretive, critical and personal.

3. Students will study immigration, pioneers and the Midwest (specifically Nebraska).

4. Students will be given the opportunity to practice reading aloud and silently to improve their skills in each area.

5. Students will answer questions to demonstrate their knowledge and understanding of the main events and characters in *My Antonia* as they relate to the author's theme development.

6. Students will enrich their vocabularies and improve their understanding of the novel through the vocabulary lessons prepared for use in conjunction with the novel.

7. The writing assignments in this unit are geared to several purposes:
   a. To have students demonstrate their abilities to inform, to persuade, or to express their own personal ideas
      Note: Students will demonstrate ability to write effectively to <u>inform</u> by developing and organizing facts to convey information. Students will demonstrate the ability to write effectively to <u>persuade</u> by selecting and organizing relevant information, establishing an argumentative purpose, and by designing an appropriate strategy for an identified audience. Students will demonstrate the ability to write effectively to <u>express personal ideas</u> by selecting a form and its appropriate elements.
   b. To check the students' reading comprehension
   c. To make students think about the ideas presented by the novel
   d. To encourage logical thinking
   e. To provide an opportunity to practice good grammar and improve students' use of the English language.

8. Students will read aloud, report, and participate in large and small group discussions to improve their public speaking and personal interaction skills.

READING ASSIGNMENT SHEET - *My Antonia*

Date Assigned	Chapters Assigned	Completion Date
	I: 1-3	
	I: 4-6	
	I: 7-9	
	I: 10-14	
	I: 15-19	
	II: 1-5	
	II: 6-15	
	III	
	IV & V	

UNIT OUTLINE - *My Antonia*

1 Introduction Speaker: Immigration	2 PVR I:1-5	3 Study ?s I:1-5 Follow-up Activity PVR I:6-9	4 Writing Assignment 1	5 Study ?s I:6-9 PVR I:10-14
6 Study?s I:10-14 Pioneers Activity PVR I:15-19	7 Study ?s I:15-19 Library PVR II:1-5	8 Study ?s II:1-5 Writing Assignment 2 PVR II:6-15	9 Study ?s II:6-15 Reports PVR III	10 Reports
11 Study ?s III Travelogue Nebraska PVR IV & V	12 Writing Assignment 3	13 Study ?s IV-V Extra ?s	14 Vocabulary	15 Language Worksheet
16 Group Activity	17 Reports	18 Review	19 Test	

Key: P=Preview Study Questions V=Prereading Vocabulary Worksheet R=Read

STUDY GUIDE QUESTIONS

SHORT ANSWER STUDY GUIDE QUESTIONS - *My Antonia*

Introduction
The introduction is an integral part of the book. What is its purpose?

Book I Chapters 1-5
1. Who is Jim Burden?
2. Who introduces Antonia to the reader?
3. What is the conductor's attitude towards Antonia?
4. What is Jake's opinion of the foreigners?
5. Identify Otto Fuchs.
6. What role does the land play in this story?
7. What are Jim's grandmother and grandfather like?
8. Chapter two provides little action. Rather, it is a portrait of a well-ordered family in a new land. Describe the Burdens' farm life.
9. Identify Peter Krajiek. What kind of a man is he?
10. What sort of home do the Shimerdas have?
11. Identify briefly Mrs. Shimerda, Mr. Shimerda, Ambrosch, Yulka and Marek.
12. Who are Peter and Pavel?

Book I Chapters 6-9
1. Why did Jim and Antonia visit the prairie dog town?
2. Describe Jim's victory over the snake.
3. Who is Wick Cutter?
4. What was the "trouble" that caused Peter and Pavel to leave Russia?
5. What becomes of Pavel and Peter?
6. Describe how the Burdens lived during the wintery, blizzardy days on the prairie.

Book I Chapters 10-14
1. In Chapter 10, the Burdens visit the Shimerdas. What is the chief motivation for their visit?
2. Describe what the Burdens find when they arrive at the Shimerda household.
3. Who has been delegated to go to town to do the Christmas shopping?
4. What prevents Jake from making his journey?
5. The Burdens decide to have a country Christmas and make their own presents. What did Jim make? Grandmother?
6. Jake and Otto also contribute to the Christmas celebration. What were their contributions?
7. Describe the finished Christmas tree.
8. On Christmas Day, Mr. Shimerda comes to thank them for the presents. What does he do to acknowledge the Christmas celebration?

Antonia Short Answer Study Questions Page 2

9. Jim wonders what his Grandfather's reaction will be to Mr. Shimerda's strange actions in front of the Christmas tree. What is Grandfather's reaction?
10. Describe Mrs. Shimerda's actions when she and Antonia come to visit during the "January thaw."
11. What information does Antonia pass on to Jim during the "thaw" visit?
12. How does Jim react to Antonia's comments about her father's unhappiness?
13. What wakens Jim on the morning of January 22nd?
14. What does Grandfather tell Jim on the morning of January 22nd?
15. Jim listens to the men talk at the breakfast table. What does he learn about Mr. Shimerda's death?
16. Otto leaves for town on their best horse, and Jim is left alone with Ambrosch. He sees a new side to Ambrosch. Describe Jim's new awareness about Ambrosch.
17. Jake and Ambrosch, Grandmother and Grandfather all leave for the Shimerdas' house. Jim is left alone in the house. How does he pass the time?

Book I: Chapters 15-19
1. Identify Anton Jelinek.
2. Where was Mr. Shimerda buried? Why?
3. How did Mr. Shimerda's death have an effect on the usual routine of the country?
4. Why didn't Antonia go to school when Jim invited her for the next session?
5. What promise did Jim make to Antonia?
6. How had Antonia changed since her father's death?
7. What caused the rift between the Shimerdas and the Burdens?
8. How did the Shimerdas and Burdens become friends again?

Book II
1. To where and why did the Burdens move?
2. Why did the Burdens see more of their country neighbors now than when they lived on the farm?
3. Who were the Harlings? Identify Charley, Julia, Sally and Frances.
4. How and why did Antonia come to the city?
5. Describe the summer life at the Harlings.
6. Identify Lena Lengard.
7. Why was Antonia reserved towards Lena?
8. In the last chapter, we learned that Lena was "talked about," and that her reputation was questionable. What do we learn about Lena in this chapter?
9. Who was Blind d'Arnault?
10. Identify the Vannis.
11. Who were the "hired girls"?
12. Why does Antonia leave the Harlings?
13. For whom does Antonia go to work after leaving the Harlings?

Antonia Short Answer Study Questions Page 3

14. What kind of a future do the hired girls, especially Antonia, see for Jim?
15. Jim is restless in this chapter. What diversions does he choose?
16. Describe the relationship between Jim and Antonia.
17. To whom did Jim dedicate his fine graduation speech?
18. As Jim talks with and listens to the hired girls talk during their summer picnic, what do we learn about the hired girls?
19. What was the "great black figure" which "suddenly appeared on the face of the sun"?
20. Why did Jim go to stay at the Cutters' house at night?
21. What was Mr. Cutter's surprise when he came into Antonia's room?
22. Why was Jim angry with Antonia?

Book III
1. Identify Gaston Cleric.
2. Who came to visit Jim at the university?
3. What news did Lena bring to Jim on her first visit?
4. To what did Jim compare the hired girls?
5. Who is Mr. Ordinsky?
6. How does Lena's presence in Lincoln affect Jim?
7. Why is Lena determined not to marry?
8. Why does Jim leave Lincoln?

Book IV
1. Why did people say, "Poor Antonia!" What happened to her?
2. When Jim came home in the summer and went to the photographers, what did he see there and how did it affect him?
3. Why did Jim go to visit the Widow Steavens?
4. How had Antonia changed since Jim had seen her last?

Book V
1. Who did Antonia marry?
2. Why did Jim wait twenty years to go back to see Antonia?
3. How was Antonia when Jim finally saw her twenty years later?
4. What happened to Wick Cutter and his wife?
5. What did Jim think of Cuzak?

KEY: SHORT ANSWER STUDY GUIDE QUESTIONS - *My Antonia*

Introduction
The introduction is an integral part of the book. What is its purpose?
    The purpose of any introduction is to set the scene, to get the reader's attention, and to lead into the main story. This is as true of an introductory paragraph of an essay as it is of an introductory section to a book.

    This particular introduction serves two purposes. *My Antonia* appears to be told to the author, Willa Cather, by a third person, Jim Burden, a childhood friend. In addition to "boxing" the story, this introduction gives the reader the nostalgic mood of the story and of the deep feeling for the prairie land. We meet two main characters, Antonia Shimerda and James Burden, and the reader learns it is not a plotted, highly structured story, but rather a tale of personal remembrance about people and places and a way of life now gone forever.

Book I Chapters 1-5
1. Who is Jim Burden?
    He is a ten year-old orphan who travels from Virginia to Nebraska to live with his paternal grandparents on a farm. He is also the narrator of the story.

2. Who introduces Antonia to the reader?
    The train conductor introduces Antonia's presence to Jim and to the reader when he tells Jim about an immigrant family in the car ahead.

3. What is the conductor's attitude towards Antonia?
    He says that the girl with the pretty brown eyes is as bright as a new dollar even though she can speak only one English sentence: "We go Black Hawk, Nebraska."

4. What is Jake's opinion of the foreigners?
    He says that Jim was "likely to get diseases from foreigners."

5. Identify Otto Fuchs.
    Otto works for the Burdens on their farm. He is fairly intelligent and can accept responsibility. He is a skilled carpenter (who later makes Mr. Shimerda's coffin).

6. What role does the land play in this story?
    The land is the antagonist. It must be controlled and made to produce. At this point in time, however, there is more raw land than that which is under cultivation. As Jim peers out at the land from the jolting wagon, he notes: "There seemed nothing to see ... there was nothing but land; not a country at all, but the material out of which countries are made."

7. What are Jim's grandmother and grandfather like?
    Grandmother is a tall, wrinkled, deeply tanned woman. She is a well-organized housewife who likes things done properly. She is friendly even to badgers, who sometimes steal a chicken and to the Shimerdas even though she does not wholly approve of them. Grandfather Burden had a snow white beard but his crown was bald and his blue eyes were young with a fresh, frosty sparkle. He was a quiet, devout man with an air of respectability about him.

8. How does each day at the Burden farm come to a close?
    Everyone, including the hired hands, attends evening prayers.

9. Chapter two provides little action. Rather, it is a portrait of a well-ordered family in a new land. Describe the Burdens' farm life.
    Grandmother's house is clean and attractive. The food is good and plentiful; the people are clean, clad well and have a deep religious faith. The gardens, barnyard and remainder of the land are well-managed. The mention of the rattlesnake is a reminder that this idyllic place, like Eden, has its serpents -- sometimes in the form of a snake, and sometimes in the form of man. This portrait later contrasts sharply with the Shimerdas' lifestyle.

10. Identify Peter Krajiek. What kind of a man is he?
    Krajiek, like the Shimerdas, is a Bohemian. He is the only person who speaks their language, and thus can tell them anything (and they must believe him). He has charged them too much for everything he has sold to them, and has generally taken advantage of them.

11. What sort of home do the Shimerdas have?
    Grandmother Burden refers to it as a badger hole. It is nothing but a shack dug into the hillside. Its roof is thatched with the red grass of the prairie. There is obviously a great deal of work to be done on both the home and the farmland.

12. Identify briefly Mrs. Shimerda, Mr. Shimerda, Ambrosch, Yulka and Marek.
    Mrs. Shimerda is the driving force in the family. She is the one who wanted to come to America. She is materialistic and ambitious for her family.
    Mr. Shimerda is an old-world man, a musician and a dreamer. He is thin and withdrawn. His skills (weaving and music) have little value on the farm. Antonia is the light of his life.
    Ambrosch is the favored child. It is to give him a better chance at a future that Mrs. **Shimerda** has insisted that they come to America. He is big and strong and should make a good farmer; however, he does have a rude temperament.
    Yulka is Antonia's little sister.
    Marek is the Shimerdas' mentally handicapped son.

13. Who are Peter and Pavel?
    They are Russians with whom Mr. Shimerda is able to converse. They seem to bring some degree of happiness to Mr. Shimerda. They have left their country because of a "great trouble."

Book I Chapters 6-9

1. Why did Jim and Antonia visit the prairie dog town?
    They went to borrow a spade from Russian Peter. On the way back, they decide to stop at dog town to see if the tunnels were straight down or horizontal.

2. Describe Jim's victory over the snake.
    While he and Antonia visit dog town, he almost backs into a large rattlesnake. Antonia screams a warning (not in English!), and after a frozen moment of panic, Jim strikes the snake's head with the spade. After Jim faces this huge trial, Antonia "never took a supercilious air" with him again.

3. Who is Wick Cutter?
    He is an unscrupulous money lender who lives in Black Hawk. He has cheated the Russians with his outrageous interest rates, and Peter cannot meet his note payment when it comes due.

4. What was the "trouble" that caused Peter and Pavel to leave Russia?
    They were part of a wedding party that was returning home after the festivities. The sledges were overtaken one-by-one by a large pack of wolves; each was overturned and the people and horses were eaten by the wolves. Finally, to lighten their sledge to be able to save themselves, Pavel threw the bride and groom to the wolves. They were ostracized by everyone. Eventually they saved enough money to come to America, but bad luck seemed to follow them.

5. What becomes of Pavel and Peter?
    Pavel died and was buried in the Norwegian cemetery. Peter sold everything and went to work as a cook at a railway construction camp.

6. Describe how the Burdens lived during the wintery, blizzardy days on the prairie.
    Next to getting warm and keeping warm, the main thing to look forward to was mealtime. Grandmother Burden pointed out quite frequently that cooks out on the prairie, as compared to those in Virginia, had very little to do. On Sundays, they almost always had chicken and the rest of the week, the meat feature of the meal was some sort of pork. The hired men suffered even more than Jim did, for no matter how cold it got, they had to go out and tend to the livestock. They often came in with their hands bleeding and cold. Saturday evenings, sitting around the fire, they sometimes had popcorn, sang songs, or told stories while the coyotes howled outside.

Book I Chapters 10-14

1. In Chapter 10, the Burdens visit the Shimerdas. What is the chief motivation for their visit?
    Otto reports that he has met Ambrosch, who asked him if prairie dogs were good to eat. Otto tried to tell him that people do not eat prairie dogs, but the boy went away with a funny smile on his face, as if to indicate that they had already eaten them. Upon hearing that their neighbors might be living on prairie dog meat, Grandfather decides that they should pay their neighbors a visit.

2. Describe what the Burdens find when they arrive at the Shimerda household.
    The first thing they see is Antonia in a cotton dress (and apparently coatless) out in the freezing weather at a hand pump. Mrs. Shimerda greets them at the door, crying. Her feet are done up in rags. She shows them two barrels; one has rotten potatoes, the other has bad flour. The house is dreadful and there is very little light (only one lantern). When Jake arrives with a hamper of food, Mrs. Shimerda weeps. Grandmother calls Antonia to help empty the basket. Grandmother learns that the two girls sleep in a hole dug into the bank and connected to the house. Finally, Mr. Shimerda tells them that he had earned good money in his old country and that he had come to America with plenty, but that somehow in the exchange when they arrived in this country, he had lost part of his money, and that the man he bought the farm from had overcharged him. Despite all of this, they still had some money left to get the farm going in the spring, but meanwhile they were having a hard time getting through the winter.

3. Who has been delegated to go to town to do the Christmas shopping?
    Jake is supposed to go.

4. What prevents Jake from making his journey?
    There is a tremendous blizzard, and Jake is unable to go to town.

5. The Burdens decide to have a country Christmas and make their own presents. What did Jim make? Grandmother?
    Jim made a cloth-covered book for Yulka and Antonia. Grandmother bakes gingerbread cookies.

6. Jake and Otto also contribute to the Christmas celebration. What were their contributions?
    Jake's contribution was to saddle-up and take the presents to the Shimerdas. Otto found nativity scene figures which his mother has been sending him all these years and he has been saving in his trunk. They are used to decorate the tree.

7. Describe the finished Christmas tree.
    It was a little cedar tree about five feet high with a very nice shape. It was decorated with gingerbread animals, the nativity figures, popcorn strings, and bits of candle which Fuchs had fitted into pasteboard sockets. There were sheets of cotton wool underneath for a snowfield, and Jake's pocket mirror served as a frozen lake.

8. On Christmas Day, Mr. Shimerda comes to thank them for the presents. What does he do to acknowledge the Christmas celebration?
   When they light the candles on the tree, Mr. Shimerda goes over to the tree, kneels down, crosses himself, and says a private prayer.

9. Jim wonders what his Grandfather's reaction will be to Mr. Shimerda's strange actions in front of the Christmas tree. What is Grandfather's reaction?
   He simply bows his own head in prayer also. When Shimerda leaves, Grandfather says that the prayers of all good people are good.

10. Describe Mrs. Shimerda's actions when she and Antonia come to visit during the "January thaw."
    She runs around the house, which she has never been in before, looking at the carpets, the furnishings, and everything else. All the while, she comments on them to her daughter in an envious, complaining tone. When she goes to the kitchen, she sees the iron pots and says that she has no fine pots to cook with at all. Grandmother gives her one. After dinner, she tells Grandmother that if she had all the kitchen equipment that Grandmother had, she would make meals just as good or better. (Hardly a gracious thanks for a fine meal.)

11. What information does Antonia pass on to Jim during the "thaw" visit?
    She tells him that her father is sad for the old country, that he doesn't look good, and he never makes music anymore. He doesn't like this country.

12. How does Jim react to Antonia's comments about her father's unhappiness?
    He very simply says that if people don't like this country they shouldn't stay here.

13. What wakens Jim on the morning of January 22nd?
    He hears men's voices in the kitchen. He feels that something is wrong.

14. What does Grandfather tell Jim on the morning of January 22nd?
    He tells Jim that there will be no prayers that morning because they have a great deal to do. He tells Jim that Mr. Shimerda is dead and that his family is in great distress.

15. Jim listens to the men talk at the breakfast table. What does he learn about Mr. Shimerda's death?
    He learns that Mr. Shimerda has killed himself. Mr. Shimerda bathed and dressed himself in clean clothes, went down to the barn, took off his boots and his scarf, lay down and shot himself in the head.

16. Otto leaves for town on their best horse, and Jim is left alone with Ambrosch. He sees a new side to Ambrosch. Describe Jim's new awareness about Ambrosch.
>He realizes that Ambrosch is a very devout person. He has not said a word all morning; he only holds his rosary in his hands, praying -- sometimes silently, sometimes out loud.

7. Jake and Ambrosch, Grandmother and Grandfather all leave for the Shimerdas' house. Jim is left alone in the house. How does he pass the time?
>At first he does chores to help his grandparents. He tries to read a little bit, but that doesn't satisfy him. Later, he starts to think about Mr. Shimerda and he imagines that Mr. Shimerda's soul is there in that cozy house where he had found some happiness on the prairie, on its way back to the old country.

Book I: Chapters 15-19

1. Identify Anton Jelinek.
>Anton Jelinek was a young Bohemian living near Black Hawk. He came to help his countrymen in their time of need after Mr. Shimerda's death. He was helpful in explaining Bohemian customs and the effect of the suicide upon the Shimerda family.

2. Where was Mr. Shimerda buried? Why?
>Mrs. Shimerda wanted him to be buried at the corner of his property where roads may be likely to go one day. Because he committed suicide, the Catholics and Norwegians would not take him in their cemeteries.

3. How did Mr. Shimerda's death have an effect on the usual routine of the country?
>People who didn't usually come out to visit came and visited and attended the funeral even though Mrs. Shimerda and Ambrosch certainly weren't the most friendly or popular folks around. People overlooked their own personal feelings and religious beliefs to respect the Shimerdas' difficulty.

4. Why didn't Antonia go to school when Jim invited her for the next session?
>She had assumed the role of being a farm hand and had no time for school even though she would have liked to have gone.

5. What promise did Jim make to Antonia?
>He promised not to forget her father.

6. How had Antonia changed since her father's death?
>She had lost her feminine ways and has less time for Jim. She had become rougher and tougher.

7. What caused the rift between the Shimerdas and the Burdens?
   Jake and Jim went to get a horse collar Ambrosch had borrowed from Grandfather Burden. Ambrosch had ruined it and didn't offer to pay for it or replace it, and, more than that, he carried a snotty, indifferent attitude about it. When Jake pulled him back to complete the conversation, Ambrosch kicked at him. Jake punched him in the face, knocking him down and stunning him. Mrs. Shimerda pressed charges against Jake for hitting Ambrosch, and the two families (with the exception of Grandfather Burden) were separated.

8. How did the Shimerdas and Burdens become friends again?
   Grandfather and Jim went to make peace with them. Grandfather gave Mrs. Shimerda the cow and told her she did not have to pay him any more money for it. Grandfather made clear that it was time to let bygones be bygones.

Book II
1. To where and why did the Burdens move?
   They moved to Black Hawk because Grandmother and Grandfather were getting too old for heavy farm work.

2. Why did the Burdens see more of their country neighbors now than when they lived on the farm?
   Because of their house's location, people used it as a place to wash and rest and keep their horses on their trips to town.

3. Who were the Harlings? Identify Charley, Julia, Sally and Frances.
   The Harlings were Norwegian farmers who had moved to town. They lived next door to the Burdens. They were important and well-off as the controllers of the grain elevators. Charley was their son who was intelligent. Sally was their tomboy daughter. Julia was their reserved daughter who was interested in music. Frances was their grown-up daughter who helped her father with his business.

4. How and why did Antonia come to the city?
   Grandmother suggested to Mrs. Harling that she should interview Antonia as a possible replacement for her cook who had to leave. Antonia came to town to earn more money for the family and to learn about the ways of a fine house.

5. Describe the summer life at the Harlings.
   Jim goes there to play with the children. Antonia plays with the children when she can. They play games and enjoy music and have a relatively carefree life when Mr. Harling is not home. When he is home, all of Mrs. Harling's attentions go to him, and the household is much more serious.

6. Identify Lena Lengard.
    She is a farmer's daughter and an old acquaintance of Antonia and Jim. She came to town to work for Mrs. Thomas, the dressmaker.

7. Why was Antonia reserved towards Lena?
    Lena had a questionable reputation. A man named Ole Benson lusted after her, and she ran about the fields in tattered and scanty clothing. She was "talked about."

8. In the last chapter, we learned that Lena was "talked about," and that her reputation was questionable. What do we learn about Lena in this chapter?
    When Lena helps Chris pick out a present for their mother, we see that she is sensitive towards her mother's feelings (as well as Chris'). After Chris leaves, she cries for him. Even though she has chosen to live away from home, she still cares for her family.

9. Who was Blind d'Arnault?
    He was a blind black man who came to the hotel one evening in the winter to play the piano. He brought warmth and excitement into Jim and Antonia's lives for a little while.

10. Identify the Vannis.
    They brought a dancing pavilion to Black Hawk one summer. They gave the children dancing lessons and the community lively entertainment.

11. Who were the "hired girls"?
    They were daughters of mostly immigrant farmers. They came to town from their farms to work. Antonia, Lena, Tiny, the Danish laundry girls, and the three Bohemian Mary's made up the group of hired girls that Jim talks about. They were free spirits compared to the town girls who were trained by their parents to be "proper."

12. Why does Antonia leave the Harlings?
    Because Antonia is getting a reputation of being free and easy like the rest of the hired girls, Mr. Harling forbids her to go to the dances anymore. Rather than giving up the good times that the dances and her friends bring her, she quits working for the Harlings so she can do as she pleases.

13. For whom does Antonia go to work after leaving the Harlings?
    She goes to work for the Cutters who have no children. Though the cutters have money, they are not of the same family spirit as the Harlings were.

14. What kind of a future do the hired girls, especially Antonia, see for Jim?
    They see a traditional, respectable future for him. The girls tease him about being a preacher, and Antonia expects him to go off to school and to make something of himself.

15. Jim is restless in this chapter. What diversions does he choose?
    He roams about the streets and goes to Anton Jelinek's saloon until Anton asks him not to come back in consideration of Grandfather Burden's feelings. Jim then decides to sneak out to the Firemen's dances even though he knows this, too, will not please Grandfather Burden.

16. Describe the relationship between Jim and Antonia.
    Jim loves Antonia but although she is very fond of him, she will not let him pursue his love for her. She wants him to go on in life and make something of himself. Their relationship is one of deep friendship. Antonia seems to want to protect him from going astray. One example of this would be her warning him about getting involved with Lena.

17. To whom did Jim dedicate his fine graduation speech?
    He dedicated it to Antonia's father, Mr. Shimerda.

18. As Jim talks with and listens to the hired girls talk during their summer picnic, what do we learn about the hired girls?
    We already know that they like to frolic and have a good time. During this day in their lives, we learn about their backgrounds -- the struggles their families have had, bits of their old worlds, their passions and deep feelings, and their determinations for their own lives and the lives of their families. This chapter rounds out their characters and shows them in many ways to be superior to the town girls.

19. What was the "great black figure" which "suddenly appeared on the face of the sun"?
    It was a plough on the horizon, magnified by the angle of the sun.

20. Why did Jim go to stay at the Cutters' house at night?
    Antonia was afraid that Mr. Cutter was "up to some of his tricks again."

21. What was Mr. Cutter's surprise when he came into Antonia's room?
    He found Jim in her bed instead of Antonia.

22. Why was Jim angry with Antonia?
    "She had let me in for all this disgustingness," he said.

Book III
1. Identify Gaston Cleric.
    He was Jim's Latin teacher, advisor and friend at the university. He introduced Jim to the "world of ideas."

2. Who came to visit Jim at the university?
    Lena Lingard came to see him.

3. What news did Lena bring to Jim on her first visit?
    She told him that she has moved to Lincoln and has set up a successful dress shop. She also told him that Antonia is as good as engaged to Larry Donovan.

4. To what did Jim compare the hired girls?
    He compared them to the poetry of Virgil.

5. Who is Mr. Ordinsky?
    He's Lena's neighbor who likes her and recognizes her weaknesses. He dislikes Jim at first because he thinks Jim is a typical young college boy out to compromise Lena. Ordinsky becomes friendly with Jim after Jim makes his intentions known.

6. How does Lena's presence in Lincoln affect Jim?
    He began to play more and study less.

7. Why is Lena determined not to marry?
    She likes her freedom.

8. Why does Jim leave Lincoln?
    Cleric has offered to continue Jim's studies in Boston, and Jim needs to get into an environment where he can concentrate on his studies instead of being tempted to play.

Book IV
1. Why did people say, "Poor Antonia!" What happened to her?
    "Antonia went away to marry Larry Donovan at some place where he was working; he had deserted, and now there was a baby."

2. When Jim came home in the summer and went to the photographers, what did he see there and how did it affect him?
    "I went away feeling that I must see Antonia again. Another girl would have kept her baby out of sight, but Tony, of course, must have its picture on exhibition at the town photographer's, in a great gilt frame."

3. Why did Jim go to visit the Widow Steavens?
    He wanted to find out the details of Antonia's experience with Larry Donovan.

4. How had Antonia changed since Jim had seen her last?
    "She was thinner than I had ever seen her, and looked as Mrs. Steavens said, 'worked down,' but there was a new kind of strength in the gravity of her face, and her colour still gave her that look of deep-seated health and ardour."

Book V

1. Who did Antonia marry?
    She married Anton Jelinek's cousin.

2. Why did Jim wait twenty years to go back to see Antonia?
    He kept putting off his visit, and after a while, he "did not want to find her aged and broken. . . ."

3. How was Antonia when Jim finally saw her twenty years later?
    "She was there, in the full vigour of her personality, battered but not diminished."
    "She was the rich mine of life, like the founders of early races."

4. What happened to Wick Cutter and his wife?
    Mr. Cutter killed his wife to make sure she died before he did so "her people" would not inherit his life's work. He shot out the window to gather attention so someone would come in. Then he shot himself. The men who came in witnessed that Mrs. Cutter had died first.

5. What did Jim think of Cuzak?
    "I found Cuzak a most companionable fellow."

MULTIPLE CHOICE STUDY GUIDE/QUIZ QUESTIONS - *My Antonia*

Introduction
The introduction is an integral part of the book. The purpose is to set the scene, to get the reader's attention, and to lead us into the main story. This is as true of an introductory paragraph of an essay as it is of an introductory section to a book.

1. How is the story told?
    a. It is told in the first person.
    b. It is told to the author by a third person.
    c. It is told in the second person.
    d. It is a combination of first and third person.

2. What is the mood of the story?
    a. It is nostalgic.
    b. It is self-righteous.
    c. It is futuristic.
    d. It is Victorian.

3. True or False: The story is plotted and highly structured.
    a. True
    b. False

Book 1 Chapters 1 - 5
4. What is the narrator's relationship to Antonia?
    a. He is her neighbor during their childhood and young adulthood.
    b. He is the son of her employer.
    c. He is her grandfather.
    d. He is the town's newspaper editor, who is writing a book of memoirs.

5. Who introduces Antonia to the reader?
    a. Jake makes the introduction.
    b. Mr. Burden makes the introduction.
    c. Another passenger makes the introduction.
    d. The train conductor makes the introduction.

6. What is this person's attitude towards Antonia?
    a. He hates all foreigners.
    b. He thinks she is pretty and bright.
    c. He sees her only as another fare.
    d. He falls madly in love with her.

My Antonia Multiple Choice Study Questions Page 2

7. What is Jake's opinion of the foreigners?
    a. He thinks they are dangerous and violent.
    b. He feels sorry for them and their hardships.
    c. He thinks people will get diseases from them.
    d. He says that anyone who can't speak English should have to return to their own country.

8. Who is Otto Fuchs?
    a. He works for the Burdens on their farm. He is fairly intelligent and can accept responsibility.
    b. He is the owner of the land the Shimerdas are renting. He is ruthless and miserly.
    c. He is the town banker. He lent money to the Shimerdas.
    d. He is Jim's guardian on the trip from Virginia. He stays on to care for Jim.

9. True or False. The land is the antagonist in the story. It must be controlled and made to produce.
    a. True
    b. False

10. Which does not describe Jim's grandmother?
    a. She is tall, wrinkled, and deeply tan.
    b. She is well-organized and wants things done properly.
    c. She has a college degree, although she never talks about it.
    d. She is friendly to animals and people.

11. Which of the following statements does not describe Jim's grandfather?
    a. He has a white beard and a bald head.
    b. He is quiet and devout.
    c. He has an air of respectability.
    d. He has a passionate love for flowers.

12. How does each day on the Burden farm come to a close?
    a. Grandfather bolts the door and blows out all of the candles. Then he loudly says goodnight to his wife and grandson.
    b. Grandmother serves warm milk and cookies.
    c. All of the family members take turns reading aloud from the latest newspaper.
    d. Everyone, including the hired hands, attends evening prayers.

My Antonia Multiple Choice Study Questions Page 3

13. Which of the following statements does not describe farm life?
    a. The house is neat and attractive.
    b. The people are clean, well-dressed, and religious.
    c. The routine lulls them into a feeling of complacency.
    d. The gardens and barnyard are well-managed.

14. True or False: Peter Krajiek is a Bohemian. He is taking advantage of the Shimerdas.
    a. True
    b. False

15. What sort of home do the Shimerdas have?
    a. They have a three-room log cabin.
    b. They have a shack dug into the hillside.
    c. They live in a tent.
    d. They live in a ramshackle old barn.

16. Who is the driving force in the Shimerda family?
    a. It is Ambrosch.
    b. It is Mr. Shimerda.
    c. It is Mrs. Shimerda.
    d. It is Antonia.

17. Which member of the family is thin and withdrawn, an old world musician and dreamer?
    a. It is Antonia.
    b. It is Marek.
    c. It is Yulka..
    d. It is Mr. Shimerda.

18. Who does Mr. Shimerda consider the light of his life?
    a. Ambrosch is the light of his life.
    b. Antonia is the light of his life.
    c. Yulka is the light of his life.
    d. Marek is the light of his life.

19. Which family member is materialistic and ambitious?
    a. It is Mrs. Shimerda.
    b. It is Ambrosch.
    c. It is Mr. Shimerda.
    d. It is Antonia.

My Antonia Multiple Choice Study Questions Page 4

20. Who is the favored child?
    a. It is Antonia.
    b. It is Marek.
    c. It is Ambrosch.
    d. It is Yulka.

21. True or False: Antonia is younger than Yulka.
    a. True
    b. False

22. What is the problem with Marek?
    a. He is mentally retarded.
    b. He is blind.
    c. He has polio.
    d. He is hearing impaired.

23. Who are Peter and Pavel?
    a. They are two traveling salesmen who try to sell the Shimerdas a lot of expensive equipment that they don't need.
    b. They are two young boys with whom the Shimerda children play.
    c. They are neighbors. They are from Russia, and Mr. Shimerda is able to converse with them.
    d. They are nephews of Mrs. Shimerda. She wants to bring them to America to live.

My Antonia Multiple Choice Study Questions Page 5

Book 1 Chapters 6 - 9

24. Why did Jim and Antonia visit the prairie dog town?
    a. Antonia wanted to get a baby prairie dog and take it home as a pet for her younger brother and sister.
    b. They were doing a research project for school and were supposed to record the prairie dog's behavior.
    c. They knew the prairie dogs were eating the crops. They wanted to try and kill as many of them as they could.
    d. They wanted to see if the tunnels were straight down or horizontal.

25. What happened to them while they were there?
    a. Antonia was bitten by a prairie dog.
    b. Jim killed a rattlesnake.
    c. Antonia fell in one of the holes and broke her ankle.
    d. They found a bag of gold coins in one of the burrows.

26. Who is Wick Cutter?
    a. He is the minister of the church in the town.
    b. He is the newspaper publisher.
    c. He is an unscrupulous money lender who has cheated Paul and Pavel.
    d. He is a neighboring farmer who has been stealing from the Shimerdas.

27. What was the trouble that caused Peter and Pavel to leave Russia?
    a. They were part of a wedding party that was returning home after the festivities. The sledges were attacked by wolves. In order to save themselves, Peter and Pavel threw the bride and groom to the wolves. They were ostracized by the others in the village.
    b. They were political dissidents. They took part in a raid on a nearby military barracks that resulted in the deaths of several soldiers. The others in their village refused to protect them and they had to hide in the woods for several weeks. Finally, they made their way to Moscow, where a group of sympathizers gave them the money and means to travel to America.
    c. They were Jews living in a mostly Christian village. The local government had been harassing Jews, and making life difficult for the non-Jewish townspeople who had business or social dealings with the Jews. The townspeople asked them to leave.
    d. They owned and operated the town mill. They had begun to cheat their customers by changing the weights on their scale. When the townspeople found out about it, they burned down the mill and drove the brothers out of town. They traveled to America hoping to make a new life.

My Antonia Multiple Choice Study Questions Page 6

28. True or False: Pavel died and was buried in the Norwegian cemetery. Peter sold everything and went to work as a cook at a railway construction camp.
    a. True
    b. False

29. Which of the following statements does not describe the way the Burdens lived during the wintery, blizzardy days on the prairie?
    a. On Sundays they ate chicken, and the rest of the week they had pork.
    b. The hired men often had bleeding hands from tending the livestock in the snow.
    c. They sat around the fire on Saturday evenings, eating popcorn and singing or stories.
    d. They spent hours each day praying and reading the Bible. The children had to commit at least one verse to memory every day.

My Antonia Multiple Choice Study Questions Page 7

Book 1 Chapters 10 - 14

30. In Chapter 10, the Burdens visit the Shimerdas. What is the chief motivation for their visit?
    a. They wanted to invite the Shimerdas to attend church with them.
    b. Grandmother was helping Mrs. Shimerda start a flower garden.
    c. Otto said the Shimerdas were eating prairie dog meat. Grandfather wanted to tell the Shimerdas that this was not done.
    d. The Burdens wanted to talk Mr. and Mrs. Shimerda into sending the younger children to school.

31 - 34. The following statements describe what the Burdens find when they arrive at the Shimerda household. Mark A if the statement is true, and B if it is false.

31. Antonia is wearing a woolen dress and a heavy coat while she is outside working.
    a. True
    b. False

32. There are two food barrels; one had rotten potatoes, the other had bad flour.
    a. True
    b. False

33. The house was dreadful and there was very little light, only one lantern.
    a. True
    b. False

34. The two girls sleep on the floor in front of the fireplace.
    a. True
    b. False

35. Who has been delegated to go into town to go Christmas shopping?
    a. Mr. Burden is supposed to go.
    b. Jim is supposed to go.
    c. Otto is supposed to go.
    d. Jake is supposed to go.

36. What prevents the shopper from making the journey?
    a. The shopper has a very bad cold and needs bed rest.
    b. The horse is sick and unable to make the trip.
    c. There is a tremendous blizzard.
    d. The family doesn't have enough extra money to buy presents because the crop from the previous summer was not good.

My Antonia Multiple Choice Study Questions Page 8

37 - 40. The Burdens decide to have a country Christmas and make their own presents. What does each person contribute?
    a. Gingerbread cookies
    b. Deliver the presents to the Shimerdas.
    c. A hand-made cloth-covered book.
    d. Nativity scene figures that were a family heirloom.

37. Which of the above did Jim contribute?

38. Which of the above did Grandmother contribute?

39. Which of the above did Jake contribute?

40. Which of the above did Otto contribute?

41. Which of the following does not describe the finished Christmas tree?
    a. It was a little cedar, about five feet high and nicely shaped.
    b. It was decorated with gingerbread animals, the nativity figures, popcorn string, and lots of candles.
    c. Jim had made a cornhusk angel to place on top of the tree.
    d. There were sheets of cotton wool underneath for a snowfield, and Jake's pocket mirror served as a frozen lake.

42. On Christmas day, Mr. Shimerda comes to thank them for the presents. What does he do to acknowledge the Christmas celebration?
    a. He kneels in front of the tree and says a private prayer.
    b. He plays Christmas songs on his violin.
    c. He kisses each of them on both cheeks, as is the custom in his country.
    d. He brings them ornaments they had made to add to the tree.

43. What is Grandfather's reaction to Mr. Shimerda's actions?
    a. He ignores Mr. Shimerda.
    b. He participates with Mr. Shimerda.
    c. He throws Mr. Shimerda out of his house.
    d. He quietly asks Mr. Shimerda to stop doing that.

44. True or False: When Mrs. Shimerda and Antonia come to visit the Burden house, Mrs. Shimerda runs around looking at things, commenting to Antonia in an envious, complaining tone.
    a. True
    b. False

My Antonia Multiple Choice Study Questions Page 9

45. What information does Antonia pass on to Jim during the "thaw" visit?
    a. She tells him Mrs. Shimerda is pregnant. Her parents are very upset, because they don't want to have to take care of another child.
    b. She tells him they are bankrupt.
    c. She tells him Ambrosch has been very mean to the other children.
    d. She tells him that her father is sad for the old country, he doesn't look good, and he never makes music any more.

46. How does Jim react to Antonia's news?
    a. He is sympathetic and offers to help.
    b. He is unsympathetic.
    c. He becomes angry.
    d. He laughs.

47. What wakens Jim on the morning of January 22nd?
    a. One of the bulls escapes and breaks down the barn door.
    b. The henhouse is attacked by a lone, ravenous wolf.
    c. He has a fever and a sore throat.
    d. He hears men's voices in the kitchen.

48. What does Grandfather tell Jim on the morning of January 22nd?
    a. Mr. Shimerda has been murdered by a thief who broke into their house.
    b. Mr. Shimerda has committed suicide.
    c. Mr. Shimerda had a massive heart attack and died.
    d. Mr. Shimerda fell through a weak spot on the ice on the pond. He drowned before the others could rescue him.

49. Otto leaves for town on their best horse, and Jim is left alone with Ambrosch. He sees a new side to Ambrosch. Describe Jim's new awareness about Ambrosch.
    a. Ambrosch is very poetic. He has been reciting poetry about life and death.
    b. Ambrosch is very strong mentally. He talks about how he will pull the family together.
    c. Ambrosch is really very kind and loving. He talks about how much he loved his father.
    d. Ambrosch is very devout. He holds his rosary and prays all morning.

My Antonia Multiple Choice Study Questions Page 10

50. Jake and Ambrosch, Grandmother and Grandfather all leave for the Shimerdas' house. Jim is left alone. How does he pass the time?
    a. He sleeps. Thinking about death is too overwhelming for him, as it reminds him of his own parents' death.
    b. He writes about the Shimerda family. He plans to make a book to give them.
    c. He does the chores, reads a bit, and thinks about Mr. Shimerda.
    d. He goes to the woodshop and makes toys for the younger Shimerda children.

My Antonia Multiple Choice Study Questions Page 11

Book 1 Chapters 15 - 19

51. True or False: Anton Jelinek was a young Bohemian living near Black Hawk. He came to help his countrymen in their time of need. He was helpful in explaining Bohemian customs and the effect of the death upon the Shimerda family.
    a. True
    b. False

52. Where was Mr. Shimerda buried and why?
    a. He was buried in the paupers' cemetery because the family did not have enough money to buy a proper grave site.
    b. He was cremated and his ashes were sent to his brother back in the old country. His brother would then add them to the family vault.
    c. He was buried at the corner of their property because neither the Norwegian nor the Catholic cemetery would take him.
    d. The Burdens had a small, private cemetery on their property. They allowed Mr. Shimerda to be buried there.

53. True or False: Although the news of Mr. Shimerda's death shook the neighbors, they did not interrupt their usual working routines to pay their respects to the family.
    a. True
    b. False

54. Why didn't Antonia go to school when Jim invited her for the next session?
    a. She had learned everything she wanted to know.
    b. The school didn't allow girls after a certain age.
    c. She didn't have enough money to buy books or clothes to wear to school.
    d. She was too busy working on the farm.

55. What promise did Jim make to Antonia?
    a. He would teach her himself in the evenings.
    b. He would somehow buy her a new dress every year until she got married.
    c. He would not forget her father.
    d. He would defend her if Ambrosch ever mistreated her.

My Antonia Multiple Choice Study Questions Page 12

56. How had Antonia changed since her father's death?
    a. She had become rude and unfeeling.
    b. She had become timid and fearful.
    c. She had become envious and complaining, just like her mother.
    d. She had lost her feminine ways and become rougher and tougher.

57. What caused the rift between the Shimerdas and the Burdens?
    a. The Shimerdas wanted Jim to marry Antonia, but he wanted to pursue his career. They blamed him for keeping her in such difficult circumstances on their farm.
    b. Ambrosch had ruined a horse collar he had borrowed. He and Jake had a fistfight when Ambrosch refused to pay for it. Mrs. Shimerda pressed charges against Jake.
    c. The local women were having a quilting bee. They didn't invite Mrs. Shimerda and Antonia because Mrs. Shimerda was so antagonistic toward everyone. She blamed Mrs. Burden for the slight, and refused to talk to the Burden family.
    d. The Shimerdas' crop was ruined by a blight. Mr. Burden offered to sell them some of his corn to tide them over. They were angry that he did not give it to them for free.

58. How did the Shimerdas and the Burdens become friends again?
    a. The minister came and talked to both families about their concerns. They finally agreed to make up.
    b. Antonia talked to her mother and Ambrosch, and then to the Burdens. She pleaded with both of the families to reconcile, and they finally did.
    c. Mrs. Shimerda had a dream where Mr. Shimerda appeared to her and told her to end the fight. Being very superstitious, she went to the Burden house the next morning and made peace.
    d. Grandfather Burden gave a cow to Mrs. Shimerda and told her she didn't owe him any more money for it. He made it clear that he wanted to let bygones be bygones.

My Antonia Multiple Choice Study Questions Page 13

Book II
59. To where and why did the Burdens move?
   a. They moved to Black Hawk because they were getting too old for farm work.
   b. They moved to Lincoln to get a better education for Jim.
   c. They moved to Black Hawk to open a hotel.
   d. They moved to Lincoln because Grandfather became a deacon in a church there.

60. What happened with regard to their country neighbors?
   a. The Burdens saw more of them because the people coming to town used their house as a place to wash and rest up and keep their horses on their trips to town.
   b. The neighbors were so disappointed and angry at the Burdens' move that most of them stayed away. The few who came only did so once or twice a year.

61. Who were the Harlings?
   a. They were the owners of the bank. They were one of the first families to move to the area, and were very snobbish.
   b. They were cousins of the Burdens. The Burdens helped them move to America from Virginia.
   c. Mr. Harling was the town doctor, for both people and animals. His wife was the schoolmistress.
   d. They were Norwegian farmers who had moved to town. They were important and well-off as the controllers of the grain elevator.

62. How and why did Antonia come to the city?
   a. She came to go to school. She was tired of farm life.
   b. She came to help Mrs. Burden for a few weeks when Mrs. Burden was ill. Antonia liked it so much she decided to stay.
   c. She became ill on the farm. The doctor ordered her to go to town and rest for a while.
   d. She came as a replacement cook for the Harlings. Mrs. Burden recommended her.

63. Describe the summer life at the Harlings.
   a. It is dull and boring. The children must do lessons for four hours each morning, then work in the afternoons. In the evenings they are allowed to play for one hour, and then they read the Bible until bedtime.
   b. Life is strenuous. The children and parents work long hours to preserve food for winter.
   c. They play games and enjoy music and have a relatively carefree life.
   d. It is very exciting. Mr. Harling takes the family with him on his business trips. When they are home, they always seem to have visitors from another state or country.

My Antonia Multiple Choice Study Questions Page 14

64. What happens when Mr. Harling is at home?
    a. He lavishes attention on the children.
    b. He expects Mrs. Harling to devote her attention to him.
    c. He ignores all of them and reads in his study.
    d. He is usually drunk, very often violent.

65. Who is Lena Lengard?
    a. She is a farmer's daughter and old acquaintance of Antonia and Jim. She came to town to work for the dressmaker.
    b. She is a saloon singer from another town. She moved to Black Hawk to try to escape her past.
    c. She is a recent immigrant from Sweden.
    d. She is a cousin of Mrs. Harling's. She came to town to be a schoolteacher.

66. Why was Antonia reserved about Lena?
    a. Lena was very confident and outgoing. This made Antonia feel inferior, and she shied away from making friends.
    b. Antonia had never had a girlfriend, and she didn't know how to behave. She wasn't even sure if it was proper for a hired girl to have friends.
    c. Lena had a questionable reputation.
    d. Antonia was simply too busy with her work to take time to get to know Lena. She decided that the endeavor was not a good use of her spare time

67. What do we learn about Lena in Chapter 5?
    a. She is independently wealthy, although she has never told anyone.
    b. She had been abused at home throughout her childhood.
    c. She has a brilliant mind, and is frustrated that, as a woman, she is not able to make the most of her talents.
    d. She is sensitive towards her mother's feelings, and misses her family.

68. Who was Blind d'Arnault?
    a. He was a gypsy fortune teller who came to town once a year. His predictions usually came true, so people flocked to him whenever he came.
    b. He was a black man who came to the hotel one evening in the winter to play the piano.
    c. He was a French cook who came to work in the town. He had an assistant who did the actual measuring and cooking, but d'Arnault developed the recipes and tasted everything. He became very successful.
    d. He was an itinerant preacher who came through town every few months.

My Antonia Multiple Choice Study Questions Page 15

69. Who were the Vannis?
    a. They brought a dancing pavilion to town one summer. They gave the children dancing lessons and the community lively entertainment.
    b. They were Italian immigrants who moved to Black Hawk. They found it hard to fit in with the Scandinavians, and after a few months, they moved to the West Coast. Before they moved, Antonia had befriended them, and learned to cook many delicious Italian dishes.
    c. They were professors from an Eastern university. They came to Black Hawk to study and write about the Midwestern farm and town life.
    d. They were the proprietors of a traveling medicine show. They tried to set up in Black Hawk, but were chased away by the town council.

70. Jim talks about Antonia, Lena, Tiny, and the Danish laundry girls, and the Bohemian Mary's. What name does he give the group?
    a. He calls them "the farmers' daughters."
    b. He calls them "the immigrant angels."
    c. He calls them "the hired girls."
    d. He calls them "the free spirits."

71. Why does Antonia leave the Harlings.?
    a. Mrs. Harling is very jealous and suspicious. She thinks that Antonia secretly loves Mr. Harling, so she fires her.
    b. Antonia misses the farm and her family, and wants to return to her former way of life.
    c. Ambrosch asks for a raise for Antonia. When Mrs. Harling refuses, Ambrosch orders her to quit.
    d. Mr. Harling forbids her to go to the dances. Rather than give up her fun and friends, she quits.

72. For whom does Antonia go to work after she leaves the Harlings?
    a. She goes to work for the Burdens.
    b. She goes to work for the Jelineks.
    c. She goes to work for the Cutters.
    d. She goes to work for herself.

73. What kind of a future do the girls, especially Antonia, see for Jim?
    a. They expect him to be a farmer like his grandfather.
    b. They tease him about being a preacher.
    c. They think he should become a professor.
    d. They think he should become a banker and stay in Black Hawk.

My Antonia Multiple Choice Study Questions Page 16

74. Jim is restless in Chapter 12. What diversion does he choose?
    a. He plants a flower garden and reads a lot about the flowers.
    b. He takes long walks in the country and begins mapping the footpaths and roads.
    c. He begins smoking and gambling.
    d. He goes to the saloon and the Firemen's dances.

75. Which of the following describes the relationship between Jim and Antonia?
    a. Jim loves Antonia but although she is very fond of him she will not let him pursue his love for her.
    b. They like each other, mostly because they have known each other for so long. Neither has any romantic interest.
    c. Antonia is in love with Jim, but he thinks of her as a farm girl, not someone he would want to marry. He wants someone more refined.
    d They are both very much in love with the other, although neither will admit it.

76. To whom does Jim dedicate his fine graduation speech?
    a. He dedicates it to his parents.
    b. He dedicates it to the Burdens, his grandparents.
    c. He dedicates it to Mr. Shimerda.
    d. He dedicates it to Antonia.

77. As Jim talks with and listens to the girls during their summer picnic, we learn about their backgrounds and aspirations. What does this information show about them?
    a. They are shallow and ignorant.
    b. They are in many ways superior to the town girls.

78. What was the "great black figure" which "suddenly appeared on the face of the sun?"
    a. It was a plough on the horizon, magnified by the angle of the sun.
    b. It was a giant scarecrow one of the farmers had erected.
    c. It was the side of a barn going up during a barn raising.
    d. It was a huge cloud of smoke from a nearby field that had caught fire.

79. Why did Jim go to stay at the Cutter's house at night?
    a. His grandmother was sick, and thought he would be better off staying away from her.
    b. Mr. Cutter invited him to dinner. Jim got drunk and was not able to get home.
    c. Mr. Cutter was out of town, and Mrs. Cutter was afraid to be in the house without a man.
    d. Antonia thought Mr. Cutter was "up to some of his tricks again".

My Antonia Multiple Choice Study Questions Page 17

80. What was Mr. Cutter's surprise when he came into Antonia's room?
    a. The door had been rigged, and a bucket of white paint spilled down on him.
    b. Mrs. Cutter and the sheriff were waiting for him.
    c. Jim was in her bed instead of Antonia.
    d. Antonia was sitting on a chair next to her bed, with a shotgun in her hands.

81. True or False: Jim was glad he had been able to help Antonia with her problem with Cutter.
    a. True
    b. False

My Antonia Multiple Choice Study Questions Page 18

Book III
82. Who is Gaston Cleric?
    a. He is a priest whom Jim befriended.
    b. He is Jim's college roommate.
    c. He is a famous writer. Jim meets him and they become friends.
    d. He is Jim's Latin teacher. He introduced Jim to the "world of ideas".

83. Who came to visit Jim at the university?
    a. Antonia came to visit.
    b. Lena Lingard came to visit.
    c. His grandparent came to visit.
    d. Ambrosch came to visit.

84. True or False: This visitor said that Antonia was as good as engaged to Larry Donovan, and Lena had moved to Lincoln and set up a dress shop.
    a. True
    b. False

85. To what did Jim compare the girls?
    a. He compared them to mountains; strong, solid, always climbing higher.
    b. He compared them to angels.
    c. He compared them to the poetry of Virgil.
    d. He compared them to prairie wildflowers.

86. Who is Mr. Ordinsky?
    a. He is Jim's landlord, a very nosy and suspicious man.
    b. He is a friend of Jim's and Antonia's. He delivers messages between the two of them.
    c. He is Lena's neighbor, who is very protective about her.
    d. He is a successful businessman who wants to buy Lena's business and convince her to work for him.

87. How does Lena's presence in Lincoln affect Jim?
    a. It makes him think more about Antonia, and he misses her greatly.
    b. She mothers him, and he is able to devote himself to his work.
    c. He doesn't really notice her, because he is busy with school and his other friends. He thinks of her as a nuisance.
    d. He begins to play more and study less.

My Antonia Multiple Choice Study Questions Page 19

88. How does Lena feel about marriage?.
    a. She wants to get married, but not until her business is stable and successful.
    b. She likes her freedom and doesn't want to get married.
    c. She is desperate to get married. She is afraid she will never find a husband.
    d. She doesn't believe in love, but says she will marry for money.

89. Why does Jim leave Lincoln?
    a. He wants to take some time off and travel to the West Coast.
    b. He is running out of money. He goes back to Black Hawk to ask his grandparents for help.
    c. He is ill and goes home to recuperate.
    d. His teacher has offered to continue his studies in Boston.

My Antonia Multiple Choice Study Questions Page 20

Book IV
90. Why did people say "Poor Antonia!" What happened to her?
    a. Antonia had gone away to marry Larry Donovan. She had become pregnant, and he had deserted her.
    b. Her husband was abusive and she was usually covered with bruises.
    c. She had been very ill, and it didn't look like she would ever get any better.
    d. She had become a saloon girl, and was not well thought of.

91. When Jim came home in the summer and went to the photographers, what did he see there and how did it affect him?
    a. He saw a picture of the Shimerdas' old house. He felt sad, and wanted to leave town.
    b. He saw a picture of all of the girls as they were then. It made him feel nostalgic about his childhood.
    c. He saw a picture of Antonia's daughter, and it made him want to see Antonia again.
    d. He saw a picture of his old farm and he wanted to go and visit it.

92. Why did Jim go to see the Widow Steavens?
    a. She was dying, and had asked to see him.
    b. He wanted to find out about Antonia.
    c. She had known his parents when she lived in Virginia. He wanted to find out what they were like.
    d. His grandparents had asked him to go and check on her because she was alone and they were concerned.

93. How had Antonia changed since Jim had last seen her?
    a. She was hard and bitter.
    b. She had grown to look and sound just like her mother.
    c. She had put on airs, and acted rather snobby.
    d. She was thinner, but had a new kind of strength in her face.

My Antonia Multiple Choice Study Questions Page 21

Book V

94. Who did Antonia marry?
    a. She married Anton Jelinek's cousin.
    b. She married a nephew of the Harlings.
    c. She married a man Ambrosch had met. He was also from the old country.
    d. She married Mr. Ordinsky.

95. Why did Jim wait twenty years to go back and see Antonia?
    a. He didn't have enough money to make the trip until his business got better.
    b. His wife was jealous of her, from the many stories he had told over the years. He waited until she died to go back.
    c. He didn't want to find her aged and broken.
    d. He had become snobbish about his success in the city and looked down on his country roots. Finally, he realized the error of his ways, and went back.

96. Which of the following quotes does not describe the way Antonia was when Jim finally saw her twenty years later?
    a. "She was there, in the full vigor of her personality, battered but not diminished."
    b. "She was the rich mine of life, like the founders of early races."
    c. "All the strong things of her heart came out in her body, that had been so tireless in serving generous emotions."
    d. "She was so crushed and quiet that nobody seemed to want to humble her."

97. True or False: Wick Cutter's wife killed him to make sure she would outlive him and have the opportunity to spend all of his money.
    a. True
    b. False

98. True or False: Jim liked Cuzak and found him a "most companionable fellow".
    a. True
    b. False

ANSWER KEY - MULTIPLE CHOICE STUDY/QUIZ QUESTIONS - *My Antonia*

Introduction
1. B
2. A
3. B

Book I Chapters 1 - 5	Book I Chapters 6 - 9	Book I Chapters 10 - 14
4. A	24. D	30. C
5. D	25. B	31. B
6. B	26. C	32. A
7. C	27. A	33. A
8. A	28. A	34. B
9. A	29. D	35. D
10. C		36. C
11. D		37. C
12. D		38. A
13. C		39. B
14. A		40. D
15. B		41. C
16. C		42. A
17. D		43. B
18. B		44. A
19. A		45. D
20. C		46. B
21. B		47. D
22. A		48. B
23. C		49. D
		50. C

Multiple Choice Study/Quiz Questions Answer Key Continued

Book I Chapters 15 - 19	Book II Chapters 1 - 15	Book III Chapters 1 - 4
51. A	59. A	82. D
52. C	60. A	83. B
53. B	61. D	84. A
54. D	62. D	85. C
55. C	63. C	86. C
56. D	64. B	87. D
57. B	65. A	88. B
58. D	66. C	89. D
	67. D	
	68. B	Book IV Chapters 1 - 4
	69. A	90. A
	70. C	91. C
	71. D	92. B
	72. C	93. D
	73. B	
	74. D	Book V Chapters 1 - 2
	75. A	94. A
	76. C	95. C
	77. B	96. D
	78. A	97. B
	79. D	98. A
	80. C	
	81. B	

PREREADING VOCABULARY WORKSHEETS

VOCABULARY - My Antonia

Book I, Chapters 1-5 Part I: Using Prior Knowledge and Contextual Clues

Below are the sentences in which the vocabulary words appear in the text. Read the sentence. Use any clues you can find in the sentence combined with your prior knowledge, and write what you think the underlined words mean on the lines provided.

1. In the red glow from the fire-box, a group of people stood huddled together on the platform, encumbered by bundles and boxes.

_____

2. Surely this was the face of a desperado.

_____

3-4. Her voice was high and rather shrill, and she often spoke with an anxious inflection, for she was exceedingly desirous that everything should go with due order and decorum.

_____

5. As we sat at the table, Otto Fuchs and I kept stealing covert glances at each other.

_____

6. His iron constitution was somewhat broken by mountain pneumonia, and he had drifted back to live in a milder country for a while.

_____

7. But, as he uttered it, it became oracular, the most sacred of words.

_____

8. Their backs were polished vermillion, with black spots.

_____

9. As we approached the Shimerdas' dwelling, I could still see nothing but rough red hillocks, and draws with shelving banks and long roots hanging out where the earth had crumbled away.

_____

Vocabulary - *My Antonia* page 2

10. Pavel, the tall one, was said to be an anarchist; since he had no means of imparting his opinions, probably his wild <u>gesticulations</u> and his generally excited and rebellious manner gave rise to this supposition.

_____

II. Determining the Meaning - Match the correct definitions to the words.

   ____ 1. encumbered   A. Not done openly; concealed
   ____ 2. desperado   B. Wise; prophetic; sacred
   ____ 3. inflection   C. Small hills
   ____ 4. decorum   D. Alteration in the pitch of the voice
   ____ 5. covert   E. Hindered; weighed down
   ____ 6. constitution   F. Bright reddish-orange color
   ____ 7. oracular   G. Vigorous gestures; body movements emphasizing speech
   ____ 8. vermillion   H. Bold or desperate outlaw
   ____ 9. hillocks   I. Physical make-up of a person
   ____ 10. gesticulations J. Appropriate conduct

Vocabulary - *My Antonia* page 3

Book I, Chapters 6-9 Part I: Using Prior Knowledge and Contextual Clues
Below are the sentences in which the vocabulary words appear in the text. Read the sentence. Use any clues you can find in the sentence combined with your prior knowledge, and write what you think the underlined words mean on the lines provided.

1. She was the only one of his family who could rouse the old man from the torpor in which he seemed to live.

2. Within a weeks all the blooming roads had been despoiled, hundreds of miles of yellow sunflowers had been transformed into brown, rattling, burry stalks.

3. He was as thick as my leg, and looked as if millstones couldn't crush the disgusting vitality out of him.

4. "You might have told me there was a snake behind me!" I said petulantly.

5. Nevertheless, I stole furtive glances behind me now and then to see that no avenging mate, older and bigger than my quarry, was racing up from the rear.

6. She liked me better from that time on, and she never took a supercilious air with me again.

7. His eyes followed Peter about the room with a contemptuous, unfriendly expression.

8. It was hard to tell what was happening in the rear; the people who were falling behind shrieked as piteously as those who were already lost.

Vocabulary - *My Antonia* page 4

9. This cabin was his <u>hermitage</u> until the winters snows penned him in his cave.

_____

10. The deep <u>arroyo</u> through which Squaw Creek would was now only a cleft between snowdrifts--very blue when one looked down into it.

_____

Part II: Match the correct definitions to the words.

____	1. torpor	A. Plundered; robbed
____	2. despoiled	B. Scornful
____	3. vitality	C. Dormant or inactive state
____	4. petulantly	D. Creek or a dry gulch
____	5. furtive	E. Haughty; disdainful
____	6. supercilious	F. In an ill-tempered manner
____	7. contemptuous	G. Pathetically
____	8. piteously	H. Retreat
____	9. hermitage	I. Vigor; energy
____	10. arroyo	J. Shifty; stealthily

Vocabulary - *My Antonia* page 5

<u>Book I, Chapters 10-14</u> Part I: Using Prior Knowledge and Contextual Clues

Below are the sentences in which the vocabulary words appear in the text. Read the sentence. Use any clues you can find in the sentence combined with your prior knowledge, and write what you think the underlined words mean on the lines provided.

1. Grandmother murmured something in embarrassment, but the Bohemian woman laughed scornfully, a kind of whinny-laugh, and, catching up an empty coffee-pot from the shelf, shook it at us with a look positively <u>vindictive</u>.

    _____

2. Grandmother went on talking in her polite Virginia way, not admitting their stark need or her own <u>remissness</u>, until Jake arrived with the hamper, as if in direct answer to Mrs. Shimerda's reproaches.

    _____

3. The cold was not severe, but the storm was quiet and <u>resistless</u>.

    _____

4. Jake was sure he could get through on horseback, and bring home our things in saddle-bags; but grandfather told him the roads would be <u>obliterated</u>, and a newcomer in the country would be lost ten times over.

    _____

5. On the day before Christmas, Jake packed the things we were sending to the Shimerdas in his saddle-bags and set off on grandfather's grey <u>gelding</u>.

    _____

6. I saw grandmother look <u>apprehensively</u> at grandfather.

    _____

7. Mrs. Shimerda and Antonia always <u>deferred</u> to him, though he was often surly with them and contemptuous toward his father.

    _____

Vocabulary - *My Antonia* page 6

8. They began to laugh <u>boisterously</u> when they saw me, calling: 'You've got a birthday present this time, Jim, and no mistake.'

_____

9. 'Well, I can take them some <u>victuals,</u> anyway, and say a word of comfort to them poor little girls.

_____

10. He was deeply, even <u>slavishly,</u> devout.

_____

11. I felt a considerable extension of power and authority, and was anxious to <u>acquit</u> myself creditably.

_____

12. He was always <u>coveting</u> distinction, poor Marek!

_____

Part II: Match the correct definitions to the words.

_____ 1. vindictive	A. Wiped out; annihilated
_____ 2. remissness	B. Anxiously; uneasily
_____ 3. resistless	C. Food for people
_____ 4. obliterated	D. Without resistance; without opposition
_____ 5. gelding	E. Free from blame or accusation
_____ 6. apprehensively	F. Loudly; lacking restraint
_____ 7. deferred	G. Negligence
_____ 8. boisterously	H. Like a slave
_____ 9. victuals	I. A castrated horse
_____ 10. slavishly	J. Revengeful
_____ 11. acquit	K. Wanting
_____ 12. coveting	L. Submitted to; gave in to

Vocabulary - *My Antonia* page 7

Book I, Chapters 15-19 - Part I: Using Prior Knowledge and Contextual Clues
  Use any clues you can find in the sentence combined with your prior knowledge, and write what you think the underlined words mean on the lines provided.

1. 'We believe that Christ is our only <u>intercessor</u>.'

___

2. Grandmother always talked, dear woman: to herself or to the Lord, if there was no one else to listen; but grandfather was naturally <u>taciturn</u>, and Jake and Otto were often so tired after supper that I used to feel as if I were surrounded by a wall of silence.

___

3. Grandfather smoothed his beard and looked <u>judicial</u>.

___

4. I loved the dim superstition, the <u>propitiatory</u> intent, that had put the grave there. . . .

___

5. She gave me a shrewd glance. `He not Jesus,' she <u>blustered</u>; `he not know about the wet and the dry.'

___

6. My schoolmates were none of them very interesting, but I somehow felt that, by making comrades of them, I was getting even with Antonia for her <u>indifference</u>.

___

7. We rode slowly, with a pleasant sense of Sunday <u>indolence</u>.

___

8. Ambrosch shrugged his shoulders and <u>sauntered</u> down the hill toward the stable.

___

Vocabulary - *My Antonia* page 8

9. Then if Mrs. Shimerda was inclined to make trouble - her son was still under age - she would be <u>forestalled</u>.

10-11. The one idea that had never got through poor Marek's thick head was that all <u>exertion</u> was <u>meritorious</u>.

12. `His sod corn will be good for <u>fodder</u> this winter,' said grandfather encouragingly.

13. `Pay no more, keep cow?' she asked in a <u>bewildered</u> tone, her narrow eyes snapping at us in the sunlight.

14. She presented them with an air of great <u>magnanimity</u>, saying, `Now you not come any more for knock my Ambrosch down?'

15. `If he slap you, we ain't got no pig for pay the fin.' she said <u>insinuatingly.</u>

Vocabulary - *My Antonia* page 9

Part II: Match the correct definitions to the words.

_____ 1. intercessor A. Spoke noisily and boastfully
_____ 2. taciturn B. Like a judge; pertaining to the administration of justice
_____ 3. judicial C. Suggestively; ingratiatingly
_____ 4. propitiatory D. Laziness
_____ 5. blustered E. Delayed
_____ 6. indifference F. Deserving praise or reward
_____ 7. indolence G. Food for livestock
_____ 8. sauntered H. Conciliatory; appeasing
_____ 9. forestalled I. Strolled
_____ 10. exertion J. Confused; at a loss
_____ 11. meritorious K. One who acts as a mediator on behalf of another
_____ 12. fodder L. Lack of care or concern
_____ 13. bewildered M. Nobleness; forgiving; graciousness
_____ 14. magnanimity N. Doesn't talk much
_____ 15. insinuatingly O. Effort; action; activity

Vocabulary - *My Antonia* page 10

Book II, Chapters 1-5 Part I: Using Prior Knowledge and Contextual Clues
Use any clues you can find in the sentence combined with your prior knowledge, and write what you think the underlined words mean on the lines provided.

1. He was a grain merchant and cattle-buyer, and was generally considered the most <u>enterprising</u>\ business man in our country.

___

2. Her rapid footsteps shook her own floors, and when routed <u>lassitude</u> and indifference wherever she came.

___

3. She could not be negative or <u>perfunctory</u> about anything.

___

4. She was quick at understanding the grandmothers who spoke no English, and the most <u>reticent</u> and distrustful of them would tell her their story without realizing they were doing so.

___

5. Julia was in the hammock-she was fond of <u>repose</u>-and Frances was at the piano, playing without a light and talking to her mother through the open window.

___

6. She walked on <u>unmollified</u>.

___

7. `I get awful homesick for them, all the same,' she murmured, as if she were answering some remembered <u>reproach</u>.

___

Vocabulary - *My Antonia* page 11

Part II: Match the correct definitions to the words.

_____ 1. enterprising   A. Reserved
_____ 2. lassitude   B. Resting
_____ 3. perfunctory   C. An expression of criticism, disappointment or blame
_____ 4. reticent   D. Showing a willingness to take on new projects
_____ 5. repose   E. Doing something with little interest or care
_____ 6. unmollified   F. Not calmed in temper or feeling
_____ 7. reproach   G. State of exhaustion or inactivity

Vocabulary - *My Antonia* page 12

Book II, Chapters 6-9 - Part I: Using Prior Knowledge and Contextual Clues

Below are the sentences in which the vocabulary words appear in the text. Read the sentence. Use any clues you can find in the sentence combined with your prior knowledge, and write what you think the underlined words mean on the lines provided.

1. While we sat in the kitchen waiting for the cookies to bake or the taffy to cool, Nina used to coax Antonia to tell her stories-about the calf that broke its leg, or how Yulka saved her little turkeys from drowning in the <u>freshet</u>, or about old Christmases and weddings in Bohemia.

   _____

2. Deep down in each of them there was a kind of hearty <u>joviality</u>, a relish of life, not over-delicate, but very invigorating.

   _____

3. She seemed indifferent to her possessions, was not half so <u>solicitous</u> about them as her friends were.

   _____

4. Guests felt that they were receiving, not <u>conferring</u>, a favour when they stayed at her house.

   _____

5. The moment he sat down, I noticed the nervous <u>infirmity</u> of which Mrs. Harling had told me.

   _____

6. She looked bold and resourceful and <u>unscrupulous</u>, and she was all these.

   _____

7. I had seen two <u>drays</u> hauling the canvas and painted poles up from the depot.

   _____

8. Now there was a place where the girls could wear their new dresses, and where one could laugh aloud without being reproved by the <u>ensuing</u> silence.

   _____

Vocabulary - *My Antonia* page 13

9. To-day the best that a harassed Black Hawk merchant can hope for is to sell provisions and farm machinery and automobiles to the rich farms where that first crop of <u>stalwart</u> Bohemian and Scandinavian girls are now the mistresses.

_____

10. On his way home from his dull call, he would perhaps meet Tony and Lena, coming along the sidewalk whispering to each other, or the three Bohemian Marys in their long plush coats and caps, comporting themselves with a dignity that only made their eventful histories the more <u>piquant</u>.

_____

Part II: Match the correct definitions to the words.

____ 1. freshet		A. Bestowing; giving
____ 2. joviality		B. Sudden overflow of a stream from a heavy rain
____ 3. solicitous		C. Immediately following; subsequent
____ 4. conferring		D. Hearty good cheer
____ 5. infirmity		E. Without a personal obligation to do what is right
____ 6. unscrupulous		F. Strong; stout
____ 7. dray		G. Attentive; careful; meticulous
____ 8. ensuing		H. Heavy, low cart with no sides
____ 9. stalwart		I. Charming; interesting; attractive
____ 10. piquant		J. Frailty; feebleness; weakness

Vocabulary - *My Antonia* page 14

Book II, Chapters 10-13 Part I: Using Prior Knowledge and Contextual Clues

Below are the sentences in which the vocabulary words appear in the text. Read the sentence. Use any clues you can find in the sentence combined with your prior knowledge, and write what you think the underlined words mean on the lines provided.

1. He was an <u>inveterate</u> gambler, though a poor loser.

2. He was full of moral <u>maxims</u> for boys.

3. He was so <u>fastidious</u> and prim about his place that a boy would go to a good deal of trouble to throw a dead cat into his back yard, or to dump a sackful of tin cans in his alley.

4. It was a peculiar combination of old-maidishness and <u>licentiousness</u> that made Cutter seem so despicable.

5. Mrs. Cutter painted china so <u>assiduously</u> that even her wash-bowls and pitchers, and her husband's shaving-mug, were covered with violets and lilies.

6. The life that went on in them seemed to me made up of evasions and negations; shifts to save cooking, to save washing and cleaning, devices to <u>propitiate</u> the tongue of gossip.

7. <u>Disapprobation</u> hurt me, I found-even that of people whom I did not admire.

8. She asked me the other day if I knew what your <u>oration</u> is to be about.

Vocabulary - *My Antonia* page 15

Part II: Match the correct definitions to the words.

____ 1. inveterate   A. Particular
____ 2. maxims   B. Unceasingly; persistently; constantly
____ 3. fastidious   C. Moral disapproval
____ 4. licentiousness   D. Having no regard for accepted rules
____ 5. assiduously   E. Formal or pompous speech
____ 6. propitiate   F. Appease; make-up
____ 7. disapprobation   G. Habitual; deep-rooted
____ 8. oration   H. Short statements of moral truths

Vocabulary - *My Antonia* page 16

Book II, Chapters 14-15 Part I: Using Prior Knowledge and Contextual Clues
   Use any clues you can find in the sentence combined with your prior knowledge, and write what you think the underlined words mean on the lines provided.

1. After my swim, while I was playing about <u>indolently</u> in the water, I heard the sound of hoofs and wheels on the bridge.

   _____

2. Antonia had the most trusting, responsive eyes in the world; love and <u>credulousness</u> seemed to look out of them with open faces.

   _____

3. She was <u>supine</u> under a little oak, resting after the fury of her elder hunting, and had taken off the high-heeled slippers she had been silly enough to wear.

   _____

4. In the afternoon, when the heat was less <u>oppressive</u>, we had a lively game of `Pussy Wants a Corner,' on the flat bluff-top, with the little trees for bases.

   _____

5. A farmer in the country north of ours, when he was breaking sod, had turned up a metal <u>stirrup</u> of fine workmanship, and a sword with a Spanish inscription on the blade.

   _____

6. In the ravine a ringdove mourned <u>plaintively</u>, and somewhere off in the bushes on owl hooted.

   _____

7. Presently we saw a curious thing: There were no clouds, the sun was going down in a <u>limpid</u>, gold-washed sky.

   _____

8. `I guess Jim could take care of their silver and old <u>usury</u> notes as well as you could.'

   _____

Vocabulary - *My Antonia* page 17

9. Grandmother said we must have the doctor at once, but I <u>implored</u> her, as I had never begged for anything before, not to send for him.

_____

10. His zest in <u>debauchery</u> might wane, but never Mrs. Cutter's belief in it.

_____

Part II: Match the correct definitions to the words.

____ 1. indolently		A. Flat-based metal loop used to support a horse rider's foot
____ 2. credulousness		B. Lending money at an excessively high interest rate
____ 3. supine		C. Gullibility
____ 4. oppressive		D. Moral corruption
____ 5. stirrup		E. Sorrowfully; in a melancholy way
____ 6. plaintively		F. Lazily
____ 7. limpid		G. Begged; asked earnestly
____ 8. usury		H. Clear; calm
____ 9. implored		I. Difficult to bear; harsh
____ 10. debauchery		J. Lying on one's back

Vocabulary - *My Antonia* page 18

Book III Chapters 1-4 Part I: Using Prior Knowledge and Contextual Clues
    Use any clues you can find in the sentence combined with your prior knowledge, and write what you think the underlined words mean on the lines provided.

1. I worked at a commodious green-topped table placed directly in front of the west window which looked out over the prairie.

   _____

2. He was, I had discovered, parsimonious about small expenditures-a trait absolutely inconsistent with his general character.

   _____

3. One could experience excess and satiety without the inconvenience of learning what to do with one's hands in a drawing-room!

   _____

4. She moved with difficulty-I think she was lame-I seem to remember some story about a malady of the spine.

   _____

5. There were chandeliers hung from the ceiling, I remember, many servants in livery, gaming-tables where the men played with piles of gold, and a staircase down which the guests made their entrance.

   _____

6. Even the handkerchief in my breast-pocket, worn for elegance and not at all for use, was wet through by the time that moribund woman sank for the last time into the arms of her lover.

   _____

7. His gravity made us laugh immoderately.

   _____

Vocabulary - *My Antonia* page 19

8. In spite of the fact that nobody ever mentioned his article to him after it appeared-full of typographical errors which he thought intentional-he got a certain satisfaction from believing that the citizens of Lincoln had meekly accepted the epithet `coarse barbarians.'

_____

9. At last she sent me away with her soft, slow, renunciatory kiss.

_____

Part II: Match the correct definitions to the words.

____ 1. commodious   A. A disease or bad condition
____ 2. parsimonious   B. Term used to characterize a person or thing
____ 3. satiety   C. Frugal; stingy
____ 4. malady   D. Distinctive uniform
____ 5. livery   E. The condition of being over-full or over-satisfied
____ 6. moribund   F. Extremely; beyond normal bounds
____ 7. immoderately   G. Giving up; sending away
____ 8. epithet   H. Spacious
____ 9. renunciatory   I. About to die or become obsolete

Vocabulary - *My Antonia* page 20

Book IV Chapters 1-4 Part I: Using Prior Knowledge and Contextual Clues
   Use any clues you can find in the sentence combined with your prior knowledge, and write what you think the underlined words mean on the lines provided.

1. Just then it was the fashion to speak <u>indulgently</u> of Lena and severely of Tiny Soderball, who had quietly gone West to try her fortune the year before.

_____

2. The photographer came out and gave a <u>constrained</u>, apologetic laugh.

_____

3. `Jimmy, I sat right down on that bank beside her and made <u>lament</u>.'

_____

4. She was so crushed and quiet that nobody seemed to want to <u>humble</u> her.

_____

5. I was <u>indignant</u>.

_____

6. She stood still by her <u>shocks</u>, leaning on her pitchfork, watching me as I came.

_____

7. She was thinner than I had ever seen her, . . . but there was a new kind of strength in the gravity of her face, and her colour still gave her that look of deep-seated health and <u>ardour</u>.

_____

8. For five, perhaps ten minutes, the two <u>luminaries</u> confronted each other across the level land, resting on opposite edges of the world.

_____

Vocabulary - *My Antonia* page 21

Part II: Match the correct definitions to the words.

_____ 1. indulgently   A. Angered by an unjust condition
_____ 2. constrained   B. A feeling or expression of grief or mourning
_____ 3. lament   C. Something that gives off light; one who is inspirational to others
_____ 4. humble   D. Sheaves of grain stacked upright to dry
_____ 5. indignant   E. Restrained; held back
_____ 6. shocks   F. Zestful intensity of feeling
_____ 7. ardour   G. Knock down a peg or two; give a lower station or condition to
_____ 8. luminaries   H. Leniently

Vocabulary - *My Antonia* page 22

Book V Chapters 1-3 Part I: Using Prior Knowledge and Contextual Clues
    Use any clues you can find in the sentence combined with your prior knowledge, and write what you think the underlined words mean on the lines provided.

1. She was there, in the full vigour of her personality, battered but not <u>diminished</u>, looking at me, speaking to me in the husky, breathy voice, I remembered so well,

    _____

2. He clenched his fists in vexation and looked up at her <u>impetuously</u>.

    _____

3. They <u>contemplated</u> the photographs with pleased recognition; looked at some admiringly, as if these characters in their mother's girlhood had been remarkable people.

    _____

4. There was a picture of Frances Harling in a <u>befrogged</u> riding costume that I remembered well.

    _____

5. I was thinking about Antonia and her children; about Anna's <u>solicitude</u> for her, Ambrosch's grave affection. Leo's jealous, animal little love.

    _____

6. `I am alive, you see, and <u>competent</u>.

    _____

7. His sociability was stronger than his <u>acquisitive</u> instinct.

    _____

8. I had only to close my eyes to hear the rumbling of the wagons in the dark, and to be again overcome by that <u>obliterating</u> strangeness.

    _____

Vocabulary - *My Antonia* page 23

Part II: Match the correct definitions to the words.

____ 1. diminished	A. Made smaller or less
____ 2. impetuously	B. Care and concern
____ 3. contemplated	C. Having a strong desire to possess
____ 4. befrogged	D. Looked at thoughtfully
____ 5. solicitude	E. Capable
____ 6. competent	F. Impulsively and passionately
____ 7. acquisitive	G. Doing away with completely
____ 8. obliterating	H. With an ornamental, looped braid

ANSWER KEY: VOCABULARY - *My Antonia*

I:1-5	I:6-9	I:10-14	I:15-19	II:1-5	II:6-9
1. E	1. C	1. J	1. K	1. D	1. B
2. H	2. A	2. G	2. N	2. G	2. D
3. D	3. I	3. D	3. B	3. E	3. G
4. J	4. F	4. A	4. H	4. A	4. A
5. A	5. J	5. I	5. A	5. B	5. J
6. I	6. E	6. B	6. L	6. F	6. E
7. B	7. B	7. L	7. D	7. C	7. H
8. F	8. G	8. F	8. I		8. C
9. C	9. H	9. C	9. E		9. F
10. G	10. D	10. H	10. O		10. I
		11. E	11. F		
		12. K	12. G		
			13. J		
			14. M		
			15. C		

II:10-13	II:14-15	III:1-4	IV:1-4	V:1-3
1. G	1. F	1. H	1. H	1. A
2. H	2. C	2. C	2. E	2. F
3. A	3. J	3. E	3. B	3. D
4. D	4. I	4. A	4. G	4. H
5. B	5. A	5. D	5. A	5. B
6. F	6. E	6. I	6. D	6. E
7. C	7. H	7. F	7. F	7. C
8. E	8. B	8. B	8. C	8. G
	9. G	9. G		
	10. D			

DAILY LESSONS

LESSON ONE

Objectives
    1. To introduce the unit
    2. To give students background information about immigrants in America
    3. To make students more aware of what it means to be an immigrant

NOTE: Prior to this lesson, you need to have contacted and made arrangements for a guest speaker to come to your class to talk with students about immigration. Your speaker should tell students what immigration is, why people have traditionally come to America, some history about immigration in America, and the process by which immigrants can become citizens of the United States.

Activity
    Introduce your speaker and give the speaker ample time to make his/her presentation. Be sure to allow time for students to ask questions at the end of the presentation.

LESSON TWO

Objectives
    1. To distribute books and other related materials
    2. To preview the study questions for Book I, Chapters 1-5
    3. To familiarize students with the vocabulary for Book I, Chapters 1-5
    4. To evaluate students reading skills

Activity #1
    Distribute the materials students will use in this unit. Explain in detail how students are to use these materials.

    Study Guides Students should read the study guide questions for each reading assignment prior to beginning the reading assignment to get a feeling for what events and ideas are important in the section they are about to read. After reading the section, students will (as a class or individually) answer the questions to review the important events and ideas from that section of the book. Students should keep the study guides as study materials for the unit test.

    Vocabulary Prior to reading a reading assignment, students will do vocabulary work related to the section of the book they are about to read. Following the completion of the reading of the book, there will be a vocabulary review of all the words used in the vocabulary assignments. Students should keep their vocabulary work as study materials for the unit test.

<u>Reading Assignment Sheet</u> You need to fill in the reading assignment sheet to let students know by when their reading has to be completed. You can either write the assignment sheet up on a side blackboard or bulletin board and leave it there for students to see each day, or you can "ditto" copies for each student to have. In either case, you should advise students to become very familiar with the reading assignments so they know what is expected of them.

<u>Extra Activities Center</u> The Extra Activities page in this unit contains suggestions for an extra library of related books and articles in your classroom as well as crossword and word search puzzles. Make an extra activities center in your room where you will keep these materials for students to use. (Bring the books and articles in from the library and keep several copies of the puzzles on hand.) Explain to students that these materials are available for students to use when they finish reading assignments or other class work early.

<u>Nonfiction Assignment Sheet</u> Explain to students that they each are to read at least one non-fiction piece from the in-class library at some time during the unit. Students will fill out a nonfiction assignment sheet after completing the reading to help you evaluate their reading experiences and to help the students think about and evaluate their own reading experiences.

<u>Books</u> Each school has its own rules and regulations regarding student use of school books. Advise students of the procedures that are normal for your school.

Activity #2
   Show students how to preview the study questions and do the vocabulary work for Book I, Chapters 1-5 of *My Antonia*. Give students about ten minutes to do the prereading vocabulary worksheet.

Activity #3
   Have students read Book I, Chapters 1-5 of *My Antonia* out loud in class. You probably know the best way to get readers with your class; pick students at random, ask for volunteers, or use whatever method works best for your group. If you have not yet completed an oral reading evaluation for your students this marking period, this would be a good opportunity to do so. A form is included with this unit for your convenience.
   If students do not complete this reading assignment in class, they should do so prior to your next class meeting.

NONFICTION ASSIGNMENT SHEET
(To be completed after reading the required nonfiction article)

Name _____ Date _____

Title of Nonfiction Read _____

Written By _____ Publication Date _____

I. Factual Summary: Write a short summary of the piece you read.

II. Vocabulary
     1. With which vocabulary words in the piece did you encounter some degree of difficulty?

     2. How did you resolve your lack of understanding with these words?

III. Interpretation: What was the main point the author wanted you to get from reading his work?

IV. Criticism
     1. With which points of the piece did you agree or find easy to accept? Why?

     2. With which points of the piece did you disagree or find difficult to believe? Why?

V. Personal Response: What do you think about this piece? OR How does this piece influence your ideas?

ORAL READING EVALUATION - *My Antonia*

Name _____ Class____ Date _____

SKILL	EXCELLENT	GOOD	AVERAGE	FAIR	POOR
Fluency	5	4	3	2	1
Clarity	5	4	3	2	1
Audibility	5	4	3	2	1
Pronunciation	5	4	3	2	1
_____	5	4	3	2	1
_____	5	4	3	2	1

Total ____   Grade ____

Comments:

LESSON THREE

Objectives
1. To review the main events and ideas from Book I, Chapters 1-5
2. To preview the study questions and familiarize students with the vocabulary for Book I, Chapters 6-9
3. To read Book I, Chapters 6-9
4. To follow-up with the introductory activity about immigration
5. To broaden students' knowledge about immigration

NOTE: Prior to Activity #3 of this lesson, you need to have gathered together a pile of magazines, newspapers, etc. with articles about immigration in them for students to use. If you don't have time to do this, you could always take students to the library/media center so they can find articles on their own. However, if you choose the library option, you may have to move the discussion of the articles to the next class period; you may run out of time in this class.

Activity #1
Give students a few minutes to formulate answers for the study guide questions for Book I, Chapters 1-5, and then discuss the answers to the questions in detail. Write the answers on the board or overhead transparency so students can have the correct answers for study purposes. Note: It is a good practice in public speaking and leadership skills for individual students to take charge of leading the discussions of the study questions. Perhaps a different student could go to the front of the class and lead the discussion each day that the study questions are discussed during this unit. Of course, the teacher should guide the discussion when appropriate and be sure to fill in any gaps the students leave.

Activity #2
Tell students that prior to your next class period they should have done the prereading and reading work for Book I, Chapters 6-9.

Activity #3
Tell students that they are each to read at least one article about immigration. Show students where to get the articles and give them time to read. When they have finished reading, hold a class discussion about the articles they have read.
This is a good opportunity for students to complete their nonfiction reading assignments for this unit.

LESSON FOUR

Objectives
1. To give students the opportunity to practice writing down their personal opinions
2. To give students the opportunity to think and formulate personal opinions
3. To give the teacher the opportunity to evaluate students' writing skills
4. To conclude the investigation into immigration for this unit

Activity
Distribute Writing Assignment #1. Discuss the directions in detail and give students ample time to complete the assignment.

If students finish this writing assignment early, they may work on the reading assignment made in the Lesson Three.

LESSON FIVE

Objectives
1. To review the main ideas and events from Book I, Chapters 6-9
2. To preview and read Book I, Chapters 10-14
3. To conclude the oral reading evaluations

Activity #1
Give students a few minutes to formulate answers to the study guide questions for Book I, Chapters 6-9. Discuss the answers to the questions in detail.

Activity #2
Give students about fifteen minutes to preview the study questions and do the prereading vocabulary work for Book I, Chapters 10-14.

Activity #3
Have students read Book I, Chapters 10-14 orally in class. If you have not yet completed the oral reading evaluations, this is a good time to do so. If students do not complete this assignment in class, they should do so prior to the next class meeting.

WRITING ASSIGNMENT #1 - *My Antonia*

PROMPT

In the last several class meetings, you have heard and read many things about immigration. One of the problems with immigration is that if too many people immigrate into one area at one time, the "system" has a hard time absorbing the people. There are many serious problems caused by floods of immigrants. Some people think we have enough of our own troubles now, that our doors should be closed to immigrants. Other people are of the opinion that all Americans are immigrants at their roots, and closing our doors to immigrants would be hypocritical and against the very principles upon which our country was founded.

Your assignment is to write a composition in which you tell what you think relating to the issue of immigration in America. Should we close our doors? Should we leave them wide open? Should there be some regulation? If so, what kind? Who should decide which immigrants will be accepted if there are limitations?

PREWRITING

Make a few notes about what you think. Write down one sentence that states your position on this issue of immigration. Why do you think that? Jot down your reasons. Next to your reasons, make a few notes of explanations or examples that support your reasons.

DRAFTING

Write a paragraph in which you introduce your main idea, your position on the issue of immigration.

In the body of your composition, write a paragraph for each of your reasons that you hold the opinion you do. Fill out the body of each paragraph with explanations and/or examples that support your points.

Write a paragraph in which you conclude your composition and give your final thoughts on the issue.

PROMPT

When you finish the rough draft of your paper, ask a student who sits near you to read it. After reading your rough draft, he/she should tell you what he/she liked best about your work, which parts were difficult to understand, and ways in which your work could be improved. Reread your paper considering your critic's comments, and make the corrections you think are necessary.

PROOFREADING

Do a final proofreading of your paper double-checking your grammar, spelling, organization, and the clarity of your ideas.

LESSON SIX

Objectives
1. To review the main ideas and events from Book I: 10-14
2. To preview the study questions and vocabulary for Book I:15-19
3. To read Book I:15-19
4. To introduce the theme of "pioneers" and to begin to examine the pioneering spirit

NOTE : Prior to this class period you should prepare your bulletin board (or flip chart or chalk board or wall) with background paper titled: THE PIONEERING SPIRIT.

Activity #1
Give students a few minutes to formulate answers to the study questions for Book I: 10-14. Discuss the answers to the questions in detail.

Activity #2
Tell students that prior to your next class period they should have completed the prereading and reading work for Book I:15-19.

Activity #3
Invite students to take markers and write on the background paper whatever comes to their minds when they hear the word(s) "Pioneer" or "Pioneering Spirit." You can do this in an orderly fashion with individual students coming to the paper, you could invite groups of five or six students to write at one time, or you could have a sort-of "free-for-all" in which all students write their thoughts down at one time.

Activity #4
After students have written their thoughts and have returned to their seats, discuss the ideas they have written on the paper. Discuss the idea that sometimes it is hard to distinguish fact from fiction in our ideas and perceptions of the pioneers of the American west. Some information comes down from history relatively accurately, but often legends and stories distort the truth as do novels, television and movies. Most pioneers were everyday, average people. Students should make a list of characteristics pioneers had to have. Some pioneers became famous or infamous because of their outstanding characteristics. Students should make a list of famous or infamous pioneers of the American west. Tell students that they should choose one famous/infamous pioneer of the American west to investigate.

Activity #5
If time remains in this class period, students may begin working on the reading assignment from Activity #2.

LESSON SEVEN

Objectives
    1. To review the main events of Book I:15-19
    2. To assign the pre-reading, vocabulary and reading work for Book II:1-5
    3. To give students time and resources to investigate their pioneers

Activity #1
    Give students a few minutes to formulate answers to the study guide questions for I:15-19. Discuss the answers to the questions in detail.

Activity #2
    Tell students that prior to your next class period they should have done the prereading, vocabulary and reading work for II:1-5.

Activity #3
    Take students to the library so they can find information to read about their pioneers. Give students the remainder of this class period to find information and read it. If students complete this assignment prior to the end of the class period, they may begin working on the reading assignment made in Activity #2.
    Remind students that this is a good activity with which to fulfill their nonfiction reading assignment for this unit.

NOTE: If you have the time or inclination, let your students really get into this assignment. Take an extra day or two. Let students dress up as their pioneers during their presentations. The West was full of colorful characters. Try to have each student do a different pioneer; otherwise you may end up with fourteen Daniel Boones.

LESSON EIGHT

Objectives
1. To review the main ideas and events from II:1-5
2. To assign the prereading, vocabulary and reading work for II:6-15
3. To give students the opportunity to practice writing to inform
4. To give the teacher the opportunity to evaluate students' writing skills
5. To prepare students for their oral reports about their pioneers

Activity #1
Give students a few minutes to formulate answers for the study questions for II:1-5. Discuss the answers in detail.

Activity #2
Tell students that prior to your next class meeting they should have completed the prereading, vocabulary and reading work for II;1-5.

Activity #3
Distribute Writing Assignment #2. Discuss the directions in detail and give students ample time to complete the assignment.

WRITING ASSIGNMENT #2 - *My Antonia*

PROMPT
You have read factual information about the pioneer of your choice. Sometime during the next few class periods you will have to give an oral presentation about the information you have read. To help you prepare for that presentation, your assignment is to write a composition in which you organize and tell about the information you read.

PREWRITING
Write the name of your pioneer at the top of the page. Make notes about the biographical information that is usually given about everyone we research: dates born and died, place born, family background, etc. Then, make notes about the life of your pioneer: what did he/she do that made him/her famous/infamous? What happened to him/her in his/her lifetime? Finally, make some notes comparing your perception of the person prior to your investigation with the facts you have found.

DRAFTING
Write a paragraph in which you introduce your pioneer.
In the body of your composition, write a paragraph for each major event/part of your pioneer's life, putting the paragraphs in chronological order.
Write a paragraph in which you tell what you thought about the pioneer prior to your investigation and comparing/contrasting that with the facts you have found.

PROMPT
When you finish the rough draft of your paper, ask a student who sits near you to read it. After reading your rough draft, he/she should tell you what he/she liked best about your work, which parts were difficult to understand, and ways in which your work could be improved. Reread your paper considering your critic's comments, and make the corrections you think are necessary.

PROOFREADING
Do a final proofreading of your paper double-checking your grammar, spelling, organization, and the clarity of your ideas.

LESSONS NINE AND TEN

Objectives
    1. To review the main ideas and events from Book II:6-15
    2. To preview and read Book III
    3. To give students the opportunity to practice public speaking
    4. To expose all students to the facts about a wide variety of pioneers

Activity #1
    Give students a few minutes to formulate answers to the study questions for II:6-15. Discuss the answers in detail.

Activity #2
    Tell students that prior to Lesson Eleven they should have done the prereading, vocabulary and reading work for Book III.

Activity #3
    Call on individual students to give their oral reports about their pioneers.

LESSON ELEVEN

Objectives
    1. To review the main ideas and events from Book III
    2. To familiarize students with the Midwestern United States, particularly Nebraska
    3. To preview and read Books IV and V

NOTE: Prior to this class period you need to have made arrangements for a guest speaker (travel agent, for example) to come to talk to your class about Nebraska and the Midwest in general. If no speaker is available, consider checking with your local AAA club, a travel agent, or a video rental store to find a good video about the Midwest. If none of these options are available, get copies of the AAA guide books for the Midwestern states, divide your class into groups, and have each group plan a presentation about each of the states.

Activity #1
    Give students a few minutes to formulate answers to the study questions for Book III. Discuss the answers in detail.

Activity #2
    Tell students that prior to Lesson Thirteen they should have completed the prereading, vocabulary and reading work for Books IV and V.

Activity #3
    Introduce your guest speaker and give him/her ample time to make a presentation. If you are not having a guest speaker, see the NOTE above and do the option you can do.

LESSON TWELVE

Objectives
    1. To review information presented about immigrants, pioneers and the Midwest
    2. To give students the opportunity to practice writing to persuade
    3. To give the teacher the opportunity to evaluate students' writing skills

Activity #1
    Distribute Writing Assignment #3. Discuss the directions in detail and give students ample time to complete the assignment.

Activity #2
    While students are working on Writing Assignment #3, call individual students to your desk or some other private area for an individual writing conference based on the first two writing assignments done in this unit. An evaluation form is included with this unit for your convenience.

LESSON THIRTEEN

Objectives
    1. To review the main ideas and events from Books IV and V
    2. To discuss the novel on interpretive and critical levels

Activity #1
    Give students a few minutes to formulate answers to the study questions for Books IV and V. Discuss the answers to the questions in detail.

Activity #2
    Choose the questions from the Extra Discussion Questions/Writing Assignments which seem most appropriate for your students. A class discussion of these questions is most effective if students have been given the opportunity to formulate answers to the questions prior to the discussion. To this end, you may either have all the students formulate answers to all the questions, divide your class into groups and assign one or more questions to each group, or you could assign one question to each student in your class. The option you choose will make a difference in the amount of class time needed for this activity.

Activity #3
    After students have had ample time to formulate answers to the questions, begin your class discussion of the questions and the ideas presented by the questions. Be sure students take notes during the discussion so they have information to study for the unit test.

WRITING ASSIGNMENT #3 - *My Antonia*

PROMPT

While you have been reading the book *My Antonia* about a pioneering immigrant family that moved to the Midwest, we have discussed immigration, pioneers, and the Midwest. Now it is time for you to put all of those ideas together. You are an immigrant pioneer who has moved west. You are to write a letter home to your cousin, also an immigrant, persuading him/her to also move west.

PREWRITING

Jot down a few notes about why your cousin should come westward. What is it about the west that would make it a good place for your cousin to live? Next to each of these things, give specific examples to illustrate and support your point.

Jot down a few notes about what objections your cousin might have to traveling westward. Next to each objection, make a few notes about how you would overcome each objection.

DRAFTING

Set your composition up in a letter format. Use whatever name you choose for your cousin.

Write a paragraph in which you introduce the idea that you want your cousin to come west.

In the body of your letter, write a paragraph for each reason why your cousin should come westward. In each paragraph use explanations and examples to support and elaborate on your reasoning.

Then write a paragraph for each reason why you think your cousin would object to coming westward. In each paragraph state the objection and fill out the paragraph by overcoming the objection. ("It is true that the trail westward is rough, but the rewards far outweigh the difficulties." etc.)

Finally, write a paragraph in which you bring forth your best arguments in a final, concluding persuasive effort.

Close your composition as a letter.

PROMPT

When you finish the rough draft of your paper, ask a student who sits near you to read it. After reading your rough draft, he/she should tell you what he/she liked best about your work, which parts were difficult to understand, and ways in which your work could be improved. Reread your paper considering your critic's comments, and make the corrections you think are necessary.

PROOFREADING

Do a final proofreading of your paper double-checking your grammar, spelling, organization, and the clarity of your ideas.

WRITING EVALUATION FORM - *My Antonia*

Name _____ Date _____

    Grade _____

Circle One For Each Item:

Grammar:	correct	errors noted on paper
Spelling:	correct	errors noted on paper
Punctuation:	correct	errors noted on paper
Legibility:	excellent	good fair poor

Strengths:

Weaknesses:

Comments/Suggestions:

EXTRA WRITING ASSIGNMENTS/DISCUSSION QUESTIONS - *My Antonia*

Interpretation

1. From what point of view is *My Antonia* written, and what effect does that have on the story?

2. Is the story of *My Antonia* believable? Explain why or why not.

3. Where is the climax of the story? Explain your choice.

4. Are the characters in *My Antonia* stereotypes? If so, explain the usefulness of employing stereotypes in the novel. If they are not, explain how they merit individuality.

5. What is the setting of the story? Could this story have been set in a different time and place and still have the same effect?

6. Explain how Antonia's appearance suits her personality.

7. Is there any humor in the story? If so, where? If not, why not?

8. In what ways is Antonia set apart from the other characters in the book?

Critical

9. Describe Jim's relationship with Antonia.

10. Are Jim's actions believably motivated? Explain why or why not. Antonia's?

11. Evaluate Willa Cather's style of writing. How does it contribute to the value of the novel?

12. Compare and contrast Antonia, Tiny and Lena.

13. Do any of the characters change in the course of the novel? If so, who and how?

14. Explain how Jim is a "town boy" even though he would prefer to be in the same set as the hired girls.

15. Explain what Jim saw in the hired girls that the townspeople did not.

16. Compare and contrast Grandfather Burden and Mr. Shimerda.

17. Compare and contrast Grandmother Burden and Mrs. Shimerda.

18. How did Mr. Shimerda's death affect Antonia? Jim? Ambrosch?

My Antonia Extra Discussion Questions page 2

19. Why didn't Jim marry Antonia?

20. Explain the influence of each of the following people on Antonia's life: Jim, Lena, Mrs. Harling, Mr. & Mrs. Cutter, Larry Donovan, and Anton Cuzak.

21. Why were the dances so important to Antonia and Jim?

22. How is this story a portrait of the coming of age of Antonia and Jim?

23. Did Antonia have a definite set of values by which she led her life? If so, what were they? If not, why not?

24. How is this story a portrait of pioneer life on the plains?

25. Compare and contrast Anton Cuzak and Jim. Why do you think Antonia chose to marry Anton instead of Jim?

26. Why does Cather have Jim compare the hired girls to Virgil's poetry?

27. How has Jim's life turned out as compared to Antonia"s? Be sure to consider information given in the introduction as a part of your answer.

28. Compare and contrast Jim's farewell to Antonia when he leaves Black Hawk with his farewell to Lena at Lincoln.

Critical/Personal Response

29. What is the value of reading a story like *My Antonia*?

30. In what ways is *My Antonia* a portrait of an era of American life gone by?

31. How could Antonia's life have been different if she had stayed with the Harlings?

Personal Response

32. Did you enjoy reading *My Antonia*? Why or why not?

33. Would you have liked to have been a pioneer? Explain why or why not.

34. Suppose this novel had been written from Antonia's point of view. How would the story have changed?

LESSON FOURTEEN

Objective
To review all of the vocabulary work done in this unit

Activity
Choose one (or more) of the vocabulary review activities listed below and spend your class period as directed in the activity. Some of the materials for these review activities are located in the Vocabulary Resource section of this unit.

VOCABULARY REVIEW ACTIVITIES

1. Divide your class into two teams and have an old-fashioned spelling or definition bee.

2. Give each of your students (or students in groups of two, three or four) a *My Antonia* Vocabulary Word Search Puzzle. The person (group) to find all of the vocabulary words in the puzzle first wins.

3. Give students a *My Antonia* Vocabulary Word Search Puzzle without the word list. The person or group to find the most vocabulary words in the puzzle wins.

4. Use a *My Antonia* Vocabulary Crossword Puzzle. Put the puzzle onto a transparency on the overhead projector (so everyone can see it), and do the puzzle together as a class.

5. Give students a *My Antonia* Vocabulary Matching Worksheet to do.

6. Divide your class into two teams. Use the *My Antonia* vocabulary words with their letters jumbled as a word list. Student 1 from Team A faces off against Student 1 from Team B. You write the first jumbled word on the board. The first student (1A or 1B) to unscramble the word wins the chance for his/her team to score points. If 1A wins the jumble, go to student 2A and give him/her a definition. He/she must give you the correct spelling of the vocabulary word which fits that definition. If he/she does, Team A scores a point, and you give student 3A a definition for which you expect a correctly spelled matching vocabulary word. Continue giving Team A definitions until some team member makes an incorrect response. An incorrect response sends the game back to the jumbled-word face off, this time with students 2A and 2B. Instead of repeating giving definitions to the first few students of each team, continue with the student after the one who gave the last incorrect response on the team. For example, if Team B wins the jumbled-word face-off, and student 5B gave the last incorrect answer for Team B, you would start this round of definition questions with student 6B, and so on. The team with the most points wins!

7. Have students write a story in which they correctly use as many vocabulary words as possible. Have students read their compositions orally! Post the most original compositions on your bulletin board!

LESSON FIFTEEN

Objectives
1. To study more closely Cather's use of the English language
2. To review ways an author can manipulate the reader

Activity #1
Take a few minutes at the beginning of class to review similes, metaphors, and personification so students will have them fresh in their minds for Part II of the worksheet.

Activity #2
Distribute the Language Usage Worksheet. Discuss the directions in detail. Give students ample time to complete the worksheet and then discuss the answers orally.

LANGUAGE USAGE WORKSHEET - *My Antonia*

In addition to using the first-person narrator to bring the reader into the world of her novel, Willa Cather's use of the English language also further weaves her world and draws in the reader.

Three ways she does this is by appealing to the readers' senses, using figures of speech (similes, metaphors, personification) and by writing many passages which say more than is actually written on the page.

The purpose of this worksheet is to have you go back an look at the text more closely to see exactly where and how these devices are used to produce the desired effect on the reader.

Why bother? Two reasons. First, it is important to know that when you read you are either consciously or unconsciously having your feelings, attitudes and opinions manipulated by the author. By recognizing the techniques of manipulation, you can begin to read more critically. Secondly, by recognizing and studying the techniques by which you are manipulated, you can begin to understand and practice how to manipulate others with your own writing or speech.

In the exercises that follow, use the whole text to find examples. THE EXAMPLES YOU USE IN EACH PART MUST BE FROM DIFFERENT CHAPTERS. Write down the example. Also note the Book ,Chapter and Page Number next to each example you cite.

Part I : Find ten examples of passages in which Cather appeals to the senses: two for sight, two for taste, two for hearing, two for touch and two for smell.

Part II: Find two examples in which Cather uses similes, two examples showing her use of metaphors and two examples showing her use of personification.

Part III: Find three passages in which the reader learns more from the passages than what is actually written on the page.

LESSONS SIXTEEN AND SEVENTEEN

Objectives
1. To further study the ideas presented in the book and the writing style of Willa Cather
2. To give students the opportunity to practice working together in small groups
3. To help students review the text and find important ideas they may have missed on the first reading
4. To give students the opportunity to practice their public speaking skills

Activity #1
Divide your class into 6 groups -- one group for each of the following topics:

1. Use of color
2. Use of the seasons
3. Religion
4. Relations between immigrant farmers and townspeople
5. Symbolism
6. Characters (Students in this group should make a complete list of the characters, describe each and explain the role of each in the story.)

Students within the group should prepare to "teach" their topic as it relates to *My Antonia*. They should find any relevant passages and come to some reasonable conclusions about their topic. One student in the group should be appointed secretary/spokesperson to write down and report the group's ideas.

Students should divide the chapters of the book among the group members so each member has to look for the group's topic within a specified number of chapters. After students have found the appropriate references, allow time for the group members to discuss their findings and come up with some intelligent statements about their findings.

Activity #2
Ask each group to report its findings and conclusions. Use these reports as springboards for discussion of each of the topics.

LESSON NINETEEN

<u>Objective</u>
   To review the main ideas presented in *My Antonia*

<u>Activity #1</u>
   Choose one of the review games/activities included in this guide and spend your class period as outlined there. Some materials for these activities are located in the Unit Resource section of this unit.

<u>Activity #2</u>
   Remind students that the Unit Test will be in the next class meeting. Stress the review of the Study Guides and their class notes as a last minute, brush-up review for homework.

REVIEW GAMES/ACTIVITIES - *My Antonia*

1. Ask the class to make up a unit test for *My Antonia*. The test should have 4 sections: matching, true/false, short answer, and essay. Students may use 1/2 period to make the test and then swap papers and use the other 1/2 class period to take a test a classmate has devised. (open book) You may want to use the unit test included in this guide or take questions from the students' unit tests to formulate your own test.

2. Take 1/2 period for students to make up true and false questions (including the answers). Collect the papers and divide the class into two teams. Draw a big tic-tac-toe board on the chalk board. Make one team X and one team O. Ask questions to each side, giving each student one turn. If the question is answered correctly, that students' team's letter (X or O) is placed in the box. If the answer is incorrect, no mark is placed in the box. The object is to get three marks in a row like tic-tac-toe. You may want to keep track of the number of games won for each team.

3. Take 1/2 period for students to make up questions (true/false and short answer). Collect the questions. Divide the class into two teams. You'll alternate asking questions to individual members of teams A & B (like in a spelling bee). The question keeps going from A to B until it is correctly answered, then a new question is asked. A correct answer does not allow the team to get another question. Correct answers are +2 points; incorrect answers are -1 point.

4. Have students pair up and quiz each other from their study guides and class notes.

5. Give students a *My Antonia* crossword puzzle to complete.

6. Divide your class into two teams. Use the *My Antonia* crossword words with their letters jumbled as a word list. Student 1 from Team A faces off against Student 1 from Team B. You write the first jumbled word on the board. The first student (1A or 1B) to unscramble the word wins the chance for his/her team to score points. If 1A wins the jumble, go to student 2A and give him/her a clue. He/she must give you the correct word which matches that clue. If he/she does, Team A scores a point, and you give student 3A a clue for which you expect another correct response. Continue giving Team A clues until some team member makes an incorrect response. An incorrect response sends the game back to the jumbled-word face off, this time with students 2A and 2B. Instead of repeating giving clues to the first few students of each team, continue with the student after the one who gave the last incorrect response on the team. For example, if Team B wins the jumbled-word face-off, and student 5B gave the last incorrect answer for Team B, you would start this round of clue questions with student 6B, and so on. The team with the most points wins!

UNIT TESTS

SHORT ANSWER UNIT TEST 1 - *My Antonia*

I. Matching/Identify

___ 1. Jake   A. Makes Mr. Shimerda's coffin
___ 2. Wick Cutter   B. Antonia's brother
___ 3. Antonia   C. Narrator
___ 4. Vannis   D. Dressmaker who does not marry
___ 5. Harlings   E. Employ Antonia; Jim's neighbors
___ 6. Cleric   F. Gets rich by a gold claim
___ 7. Jim   G. Hits Ambrosch, causing a little feud
___ 8. Martha   H. Greedy usurer, employs Antonia
___ 9. Ambrosch   I. Deserts Antonia
___ 10. Lena   J. Bring dance to Black Hawk
___ 11. Otto   K. Lena's neighbor
___ 12. Larry Donovan   L. Antonia's first baby
___ 13. Cuzak   M. Jim's life-long friend
___ 14. Ordinsky   N. Jim's advisor and teacher
___ 15. Tiny   O. Marries Antonia

II. Short Answer

1. Describe Jim's victory over the snake.

2. Describe how the Burdens lived during the wintery, blizzardy days on the prairie.

3. Jim wonders what his Grandfather's reaction will be to Mr. Shimerda's strange actions in front of the Christmas tree. What is Grandfather's reaction?

Antonia Short Answer Unit Test 1 Page 2

4. Jim listens to the men talk at the breakfast table. What does he learn about Mr. Shimerda's death?

5. How did Mr. Shimerda's death have an effect on the usual routine of the country?

6. To where and why did the Burdens move?

7. How and why did Antonia come to the town?

8. Who were the "hired girls"?

9. Why does Antonia leave the Harlings?

10. Describe the relationship between Jim and Antonia.

11. How does Lena's presence in Lincoln affect Jim?

12. Why did people say, "Poor Antonia!" What happened to her?

13. How was Antonia when Jim finally saw her twenty years later?

Antonia Short Answer Unit Test 1 Page 3

III. Essay

    It has been said that Antonia is a symbol for the earth and for motherhood. Using specific examples from the text, explain how this statement could be true.

Antonia Short Answer Unit Test 1 Page 4

IV. Vocabulary

Listen to the vocabulary words and write them down. Go back later and fill in the correct definition for each word.

1.

2.

3.

4.

5.

6.

7.

8.

9.

10.

SHORT ANSWER UNIT TEST 2 - *My Antonia*

I. Matching
- ___ 1. Jake
- ___ 2. Wick Cutter
- ___ 3. Antonia
- ___ 4. Vannis
- ___ 5. Harlings
- ___ 6. Cleric
- ___ 7. Jim
- ___ 8. Martha
- ___ 9. Ambrosch
- ___ 10. Lena
- ___ 11. Otto
- ___ 12. Larry Donovan
- ___ 13. Cuzak
- ___ 14. Ordinsky
- ___ 15. Tiny
- ___ 16. Burden
- ___ 17. Cather
- ___ 18. Steavens

A. Employ Antonia; Jim's neighbors
B. Marries Antonia
C. Jim went to see this widow
D. Gets rich by a gold claim
E. Makes Mr. Shimerda's coffin
F. Dressmaker who does not marry
G. Author
H. Jim's last name
I. Jim's advisor and teacher
J. Deserts Antonia
K. Antonia's first baby
L. Lena's neighbor
M. Jim's life-long friend
N. Bring dance to Black Hawk
O. Antonia's brother
P. Greedy usurer, employs Antonia
Q. Hits Ambrosch, causing a little feud
R. Narrator

II. Short Answer

1. What role does the land play in this story?

2. What sort of home do the Shimerdas have?

Antonia Short Answer Unit Test 2 Page 2

3. Describe how the Burdens lived during the wintery, blizzardy days on the prairie.

4. Describe what the Burdens find when they arrive at the Shimerda household.

5. Jim listens to the men talk at the breakfast table. What does he learn about Mr. Shimerda's death?

6. How did Mr. Shimerda's death have an effect on the usual routine of the country?

7. What caused the rift between the Shimerdas and the Burdens?

8. How and why did Antonia come to the city?

9. Why does Antonia leave the Harlings?

10. Describe the relationship between Jim and Antonia.

11. How does Lena's presence in Lincoln affect Jim?

12. How had Antonia changed since Jim had seen her last?

Antonia Short Answer Unit Test 2 Page 3

III. Composition

1. Explain what Jim saw in the hired girls that the townspeople did not.

2. Compare and contrast Grandfather Burden and Mr. Shimerda.

3. Why didn't Jim and Antonia get married?

4. What effect did Mr. & Mrs. Cutter have on Antonia's life?

Antonia Short Answer Unit Test 2 Page 4

IV. Essay

What are we to gain from reading *My Antonia*? What point do you think the author had in mind when she wrote the book?

IV. Vocabulary

Listen to the vocabulary words and write them down. Go back later and fill in the correct definition for each word.

1.

2.

3.

4.

5.

6.

7.

8.

9.

10.

KEY: SHORT ANSWER UNIT TESTS - *My Antonia*

The short answer questions are taken directly from the study guides.
If you need to look up the answers, you will find them in the study guide section.

Answers to the composition questions will vary depending on your
class discussions and the level of your students.

For the vocabulary section of the test, choose ten of the
words from the vocabulary lists to read orally for your students.

The answers to the matching section of the test are below.

Answers to the matching section of the Advanced Short Answer Unit Test
are the same as for Short Answer Unit Test #2.

Test #1	Test #2
1. G	1. O
2. H	2. P
3. M	3. M
4. J	4. N
5. E	5. A
6. N	6. I
7. C	7. R
8. L	8. K
9. B	9. O
10. D	10. F
11. A	11. E
12. I	12. J
13. O	13. B
14. K	14. L
15. F	15. D
	16. H
	17. G
	18. C

ADVANCED SHORT ANSWER UNIT TEST - *My Antonia*

I. Matching

    ___ 1. Jake   A. Employ Antonia; Jim's neighbors
    ___ 2. Wick Cutter   B. Marries Antonia
    ___ 3. Antonia   C. Jim went to see this widow
    ___ 4. Vannis   D. Gets rich by a gold claim
    ___ 5. Harlings   E. Makes Mr. Shimerda's coffin
    ___ 6. Cleric   F. Dressmaker who does not marry
    ___ 7. Jim   G. Author
    ___ 8. Martha   H. Jim's last name
    ___ 9. Ambrosch   I. Jim's advisor and teacher
    ___ 10. Lena   J. Deserts Antonia
    ___ 11. Otto   K. Antonia's first baby
    ___ 12. Larry Donovan   L. Lena's neighbor
    ___ 13. Cuzak   M. Jim's life-long friend
    ___ 14. Ordinsky   N. Bring dance to Black Hawk
    ___ 15. Tiny   O. Antonia's brother
    ___ 16. Burden   P. Greedy usurer, employs Antonia
    ___ 17. Cather   Q. Hits Ambrosch, causing a little feud
    ___ 18. Steavens   R. Narrator

II. Short Answer

1. From what point of view is *My Antonia* written, and what effect does that have on the story?

2. Describe Jim's relationship with Antonia.

3. Compare and contrast Antonia, Tiny and Lena.

Antonia Advanced Short Answer Unit Test Page 2

4. Explain how Jim is a "town boy" even though he would prefer to be in the same set as the hired girls.

5. Explain what Jim saw in the hired girls that the townspeople did not.

6. Compare and contrast Grandfather Burden and Mr. Shimerda.

7. How did Mr. Shimerda's death affect Antonia? Jim? Ambrosch?

8. Why didn't Jim marry Antonia?

Antonia Advanced Short Answer Unit Test Page 3

9. Explain the influence of each of the following people on Antonia's life: Jim, Lena, Mrs. Harling, Mr. & Mrs. Cutter, Larry Donovan, and Anton Cuzak.

10. Compare and contrast Anton Cuzak and Jim. Why do you think Antonia chose to marry Anton instead of Jim?

11. Compare and contrast Jim's farewell to Antonia when he leaves Black Hawk with his farewell to Lena at Lincoln.

Antonia Advanced Short Answer Unit Test Page 4

III. Composition
    Explain how *My Antonia* is a realistic portrait of pioneer life.

Antonia Advanced Short Answer Unit Test Page 5

III. Vocabulary

    Write down the vocabulary words you are given. Go back later and use all of those vocabulary words in a composition relating to *My Antonia*.

MULTIPLE CHOICE UNIT TEST 1 - *My Antonia*

I. Matching/Identify

___ 1. Jake   A. Makes Mr. Shimerda's coffin
___ 2. Wick Cutter   B. Antonia's brother
___ 3. Antonia   C. Narrator
___ 4. Vannis   D. Dressmaker who does not marry
___ 5. Harlings   E. Employ Antonia; Jim's neighbors
___ 6. Cleric   F. Gets rich by a gold claim
___ 7. Jim   G. Hits Ambrosch, causing a little feud
___ 8. Martha   H. Greedy usurer, employs Antonia
___ 9. Ambrosch   I. Deserts Antonia
___ 10. Lena   J. Bring dance to Black Hawk
___ 11. Otto   K. Lena's neighbor
___ 12. Larry Donovan   L. Antonia's first baby
___ 13. Cuzak   M. Jim's life-long friend
___ 14. Ordinsky   N. Jim's advisor and teacher
___ 15. Tiny   O. Marries Antonia

II. Multiple Choice

1. In Chapter 10, the Burdens visit the Shimerdas. What is the chief motivation for their visit?
    a. They wanted to invite the Shimerdas to attend church with them.
    b. Grandmother was helping Mrs. Shimerda start a flower garden.
    c. Otto said the Shimerdas were eating prairie dog meat. Grandfather wanted to tell the Shimerdas that this was not done.
    d. The Burdens wanted to talk Mr. and Mrs. Shimerda into sending the younger children to school.

2. What does Grandfather tell Jim on the morning of January 22nd?
    a. Mr. Shimerda has been murdered by a thief who broke into their house.
    b. Mr. Shimerda has committed suicide.
    c. Mr. Shimerda had a massive heart attck and died.
    d. Mr. Shimerda fell through a weak spot on the ice on the pond. He drowned before the others could rescue him.

Antonia Multiple Choice Unit Test 1 Page 2

3. Where was Mr. Shimerda buried and why?
    a. He was buried in the paupers' cemetery because the family did not have enough money to buy a proper grave site.
    b. He was cremated and his ashes were sent to his brother back in the old country. His brother would then add them to the family vault.
    c. He was buried at the corner of their property because neither the Norwegian nor the Catholic cemetery would take him.
    d. The Burdens had a small, private cemetery on their property. They allowed Mr. Shimerda to be buried there.

4. What caused the rift between the Shimerdas and the Burdens?
    a. The Shimerdas wanted Jim to marry Antonia, but he wanted to pursue his career. They blamed him for keeping her in such difficult circumstances on their farm.
    b. Ambrosch had ruined a horse collar he had borrowed. He and Jake had a fistfight when Ambrosch refused to pay for it. Mrs. Shimerda pressed charges against Jake.
    c. The local women were having a quilting bee. They didn't invite Mrs. Shimerda and Antonia because Mrs. Shimerda was so antagonistic toward everyone. She blamed Mrs. Burden for the slight, and refused to talk to the Burden family.
    d. The Shimerdas' crop was ruined by a blight. Mr. Burden offered to sell them some of his corn to tide them over. They were angry that he did not give it to them for free.

5. To where and why did the Burdens move?
    a. They moved to Black Hawk because they were getting too old for farm work.
    b. They moved to Lincoln to get a better education for Jim.
    c. They moved to Black Hawk to open a hotel.
    d. They moved to Lincoln because Grandfather became a deacon in a church there.

6. How and why did Antonia come to the city?
    a. She came to go to school. She was tired of farm life.
    b. She came to help Mrs. Burden for a few weeks when Mrs. Burden was ill. Antonia liked it so much she decided to stay.
    c. She became ill on the farm. The doctor ordered her to go to town and rest for a while.
    d. She came as a replacement cook for the Harlings. Mrs. Burden recommended her.

7. Which of the following describes the relationship between Jim and Antonia?
    a. Jim loves Antonia but although she is very fond of him she will not let him pursue his love for her.
    b. They like each other, mostly because they have known each other for so long. Neither has any romantic interest.
    c. Antonia is in love with Jim, but he thinks of her as a farm girl, not someone he would want to marry. He wants someone more refined.
    d They are both very much in love with the other, although neither will admit it.

Antonia Multiple Choice Unit Test 1 Page 3

8. How does Lena's presence in Lincoln affect Jim?
    a. It makes him think more about Antonia, and he misses her greatly.
    b. She mothers him, and he is able to devote himself to his work.
    c. He doesn't really notice her, because he is busy with school and his other friends. He thinks of her as a nuisance.
    d. He begins to play more and study less.

9. Which of the following quotes does <u>not</u> describe the way Antonia was when Jim finally saw her twenty years later?
    a. "She was there, in the full vigor of her personality, battered but not diminished."
    b. "She was the rich mine of life, like the founders of early races."
    c. "All the strong things of her heart came out in her body, that had been so tireless in serving generous emotions."
    d. "She was so crushed and quiet that nobody seemed to want to humble her."

My Antonia Multiple Choice Unit Test 1 Page 4

III. Composition
    Compare and contrast the Burden family with the Shimerda family.

Antonia Multiple Choice Unit Test Page 5

IV. Vocabulary - Match the correct definitions to the words.

____ 1. PITEOUSLY   A. Wise; prophetic; sacred

____ 2. FODDER   B. Knock down a peg or two; give a lower station or condition to

____ 3. PLAINTIVELY   C. A feeling or expression of grief or mourning

____ 4. INDIGNANT   D. Shifty; stealthy

____ 5. CONSTITUTION   E. Angered by an unjust condition

____ 6. PIQUANT   F. Nobleness; forgivingness; graciousness

____ 7. CREDULOUSNESS   G. Confused; at a loss

____ 8. LASSITUDE   H. Restrained; held back

____ 9. HILLOCKS   I. Something that gives off light

____ 10. JOVIALITY   J. Zestful intensity of feeling

____ 11. MAGNANIMITY   K. Pathetically

____ 12. LAMENT   L. Charming; interesting; attraction

____ 13. CONSTRAINED   M. Small hills

____ 14. HUMBLE   N. Sorrowfully; in a melancholy way

____ 15. ARDOUR   O. Food for livestock

____ 16. IMMODERATELY   P. Extremely; beyond normal bounds

____ 17. FURTIVE   Q. State of exhaustion or inactivity

____ 18. LUMINARIES   R. Hearty good cheer

____ 19. BEWILDERED   S. Physical makeup of a person

____ 20. ORACULAR   T. Gullibility

MULTIPLE CHOICE UNIT TEST 2 - *My Antonia*

I. Matching

___ 1. Jake
___ 2. Wick Cutter
___ 3. Antonia
___ 4. Vannis
___ 5. Harlings
___ 6. Cleric
___ 7. Jim
___ 8. Martha
___ 9. Ambrosch
___ 10. Lena
___ 11. Otto
___ 12. Larry Donovan
___ 13. Cuzak
___ 14. Ordinsky
___ 15. Tiny
___ 16. Burden
___ 17. Cather
___ 18. Steavens

A. Employ Antonia; Jim's neighbors
B. Marries Antonia
C. Jim went to see this widow
D. Gets rich by a gold claim
E. Makes Mr. Shimerda's coffin
F. Dressmaker who does not marry
G. Author
H. Jim's last name
I. Jim's advisor and teacher
J. Deserts Antonia
K. Antonia's first baby
L. Lena's neighbor
M. Jim's life-long friend
N. Bring dance to Black Hawk
O. Antonia's brother
P. Greedy usurer, employs Antonia
Q. Hits Ambrosch, causing a little feud
R. Narrator

II. Multiple Choice

1. In Chapter 10, the Burdens visit the Shimerdas. What is the chief motivation for their visit?
    a. Otto said the Shimerdas were eating prairie dog meat. Grandfather wanted to tell the Shimerdas that this was not done.
    b. Grandmother was helping Mrs. Shimerda start a flower garden.
    c. They wanted to invite the Shimerdas to attend church with them.
    d. The Burdens wanted to talk Mr. and Mrs. Shimerda into sending the younger children to school.

2. What does Grandfather tell Jim on the morning of January 22nd?
    a. Mr. Shimerda has been murdered by a thief who broke into their house.
    b. Mr. Shimerda had a massive heart attck and died.
    c. Mr. Shimerda has committed suicide.
    d. Mr. Shimerda fell through a weak spot on the ice on the pond. He drowned before the others could rescue him.

Antonia Multiple Choice Unit Test 2 Page 2

3. Where was Mr. Shimerda buried and why?
    a. He was buried in the paupers' cemetery because the family did not have enough money to buy a proper grave site.
    b. He was cremated and his ashes were sent to his brother back in the old country. His brother would then add them to the family vault.
    c. The Burdens had a small, private cemetery on their property. They allowed Mr. Shimerda to be buried there.
    d. He was buried at the corner of their property because neither the Norwegian nor the Catholic cemetery would take him.

4. What caused the rift between the Shimerdas and the Burdens?
    a. The Shimerdas wanted Jim to marry Antonia, but he wanted to pursue his career. They blamed him for keeping her in such difficult circumstances on their farm.
    b. The local women were having a quilting bee. They didn't invite Mrs. Shimerda and Antonia because Mrs. Shimerda was so antagonistic toward everyone. She blamed Mrs. Burden for the slight, and refused to talk to the Burden family.
    c. Ambrosch had ruined a horse collar he had borrowed. He and Jake had a fistfight when Ambrosch refused to pay for it. Mrs. Shimerda pressed charges against Jake.
    d. The Shimerdas' crop was ruined by a blight. Mr. Burden offered to sell them some of his corn to tide them over. They were angry that he did not give it to them for free.

5. To where and why did the Burdens move?
    a. They moved to Black Hawk to open a hotel.
    b. They moved to Lincoln to get a better education for Jim.
    c. They moved to Black Hawk because they were getting too old for farm work.
    d. They moved to Lincoln because Grandfather became a deacon in a church there.

6. How and why did Antonia come to the city?
    a. She came as a replacement cook for the Harlings.
    b. She came to help Mrs. Burden for a few weeks when Mrs. Burden was ill. Antonia liked it so much she decided to stay.
    c. She became ill on the farm. The doctor ordered her to go to town and rest for a while.
    d. She came to go to school. She was tired of farm life.

7. Which of the following describes the relationship between Jim and Antonia?
    a. Antonia is in love with Jim, but he thinks of her as a farm girl, not someone he would want to marry. He wants someone more refined.
    b. They like each other, mostly because they have known each other for so long. Neither has any romantic interest.
    c. Jim loves Antonia but although she will not let him pursue his love for her.
    d They are both very much in love with the other, although neither will admit it.

Antonia Multiple Choice Unit Test 2 Page 3

8. How does Lena's presence in Lincoln affect Jim?
   a. It makes him think more about Antonia, and he misses her greatly.
   b. He begins to play more and study less.
   c. He doesn't really notice her, because he is busy with school and his other friends. He thinks of her as a nuisance.
   d. She mothers him, and he is able to devote himself to his work.

9. Which of the following quotes does not describe the way Antonia was when Jim finally saw her twenty years later?
   a. "She was there, in the full vigor of her personality, battered but not diminished."
   b. "She was the rich mine of life, like the founders of early races."
   c. "She was so crushed and quiet that nobody seemed to want to humble her."
   d. "All the strong things of her heart came out in her body, that had been so tireless in serving generous emotions."

Antonia Multiple Choice Unit Test 2 Page 4

III. Composition

    Explain how the elements of immigration, pioneer life and life on the plains come together in *My Antonia*.

Antonia Multiple Choice Unit Test 2 Page 5

IV. Vocabulary - Match the correct definitions to the words.

____ 1. DEBAUCHERY   A. Frailty; feebleness; weakness

____ 2. DEFERRED   B. Strong; stout

____ 3. LASSITUDE   C. Not done openly; at least partially concealed

____ 4. ORATION   D. Formal speech; pompous speech

____ 5. FODDER   E. Plundered; robbed

____ 6. FASTIDIOUS   F. State of exhaustion or inactivity

____ 7. SLAVISHLY   G. Wanting

____ 8. ARDOUR   H. A feeling or expression of grief or mourning

____ 9. COVERT   I. A heavy cart without sides

____ 10. OBLITERATED   J. Wiped out; annihilated

____ 11. SUPINE   K. Laziness

____ 12. LAMENT   L. Not calmed in temper or feeling

____ 13. DRAY   M. Moral corruption

____ 14. TORPOR   N. Particular

____ 15. UNMOLLIFIED   O. Zestful intensity of feeling

____ 16. DESPOILED   P. Submitted to; gave in to

____ 17. STALWART   Q. Dormant or inactive state

____ 18. INDOLENCE   R. Food for livestock

____ 19. INFIRMITY   S. Like a slave

____ 20. COVETING   T. Lying on one's back

ANSWER SHEET - *My Antonia*
Multiple Choice Unit Tests

I. Matching	II. Multiple Choice	IV. Vocabulary
1. ___	1. ___	1. ___
2. ___	2. ___	2. ___
3. ___	3. ___	3. ___
4. ___	4. ___	4. ___
5. ___	5. ___	5. ___
6. ___	6. ___	6. ___
7. ___	7. ___	7. ___
8. ___	8. ___	8. ___
9. ___	9. ___	9. ___
10. ___		10. ___
11. ___		11. ___
12. ___		12. ___
13. ___		13. ___
14. ___		14. ___
15. ___		15. ___
16. ___		16. ___
17. ___		17. ___
18. ___		18. ___
		19. ___
		20. ___

ANSWER KEY - *My Antonia*
Multiple Choice Unit Tests

Answers to Unit Test 1 are in the left column. Answers to Unit Test 2 are in the right column.

I. Matching	II. Multiple Choice	IV. Vocabulary
1. G O	1. C A	1. K M
2. H P	2. B C	2. O P
3. M M	3. C D	3. N F
4. J N	4. B C	4. E D
5. E A	5. A C	5. S R
6. N I	6. D A	6. L N
7. C R	7. A C	7. T S
8. L K	8. D B	8. Q O
9. B O	9. D C	9. M C
10. D F		10. R J
11. A E		11. F T
12. I J		12. C H
13. O B		13. H I
14. K L		14. B Q
15. P D		15. J L
16. - H		16. P E
17. - G		17. D B
18. - C		18. I K
		19. G A
		20. A G

UNIT RESOURCE MATERIALS

BULLETIN BOARD IDEAS - *My Antonia*

1. Save one corner of the board for the best of students' *My Antonia* writing assignments.

2. Take one of the word search puzzles from the extra activities section and with a marker copy it over in a large size on the bulletin board. Write the clue words to find to one side. Invite students prior to and after class to find the words and circle them on the bulletin board.

3. Write several of the most significant quotations from the book onto the board on brightly colored paper.

4. Make a bulletin board listing the vocabulary words for this unit. As you complete sections of the novel and discuss the vocabulary for each section, write the definitions on the bulletin board. (If your board is one students face frequently, it will help them learn the words.)

5. Use the bulletin board suggested in Lesson Six.

6. Title the board PIONEERS. Post pictures of various famous/infamous pioneers. When students get to Lessons Seven and/or Eight, have students identify each of the pioneers. After the writing assignments are done post the informative biographical information about each pioneer on your bulletin board.

7. Post pictures of pioneer life.

8. Make a travel bulletin board showing a map and many of the sights to see in the Midwest.

9. Make a bulletin board about the immigration theme, showing pictures of immigrants and telling what immigrants have to do to get citizenship.

10. Make a bulletin board centered around the Language Usage Worksheet, giving examples of Willa Cather's use of the language. You can create this bulletin board in Lesson Fifteen as you discuss the answers to the worksheet.

EXTRA ACTIVITIES

One of the difficulties in teaching a novel is that all students don't read at the same speed. One student who likes to read may take the book home and finish it in a day or two. Sometimes a few students finish the in-class assignments early. The problem, then, is finding suitable extra activities for students.

The best thing I've found is to keep a little library in the classroom. For this unit on *My Antonia,* you might check out from the school library other related books and articles about farming, life on the plains, pioneers, immigration, or careers in agriculture, dance, music or sewing. You might also include other works by Willa Cather and articles about *My Antonia*.

Other things you may keep on hand are puzzles. We have made some relating directly to *My Antonia* for you. Feel free to duplicate them.

Some students may like to draw. You might devise a contest or allow some extra-credit grade for students who draw characters or scenes from *My Antonia*. Note, too, that if the students do not want to keep their drawings you may pick up some extra bulletin board materials this way. If you have a contest and you supply the prize (a CD or something like that perhaps), you could, possibly, make the drawing itself a non-refundable entry fee.

The pages which follow contain games, puzzles and worksheets. The keys, when appropriate, immediately follow the puzzle or worksheet. There are two main groups of activities: one group for the unit; that is, generally relating to the *My Antonia* text, and another group of activities related strictly to *My Antonia* vocabulary.

Directions for these games, puzzles and worksheets are self-explanatory. The object here is to provide you with extra materials you may use in any way you choose.

MORE ACTIVITIES - *My Antonia*

1. Pick a chapter or scene with a great deal of dialogue and have the students act it out on a stage. (Perhaps you could assign various scenes to different groups of students so more than one scene could be acted and more students could participate.)

2. Have students design a book cover (front and back and inside flaps) for *My Antonia*.

3. Have students design a bulletin board (ready to be put up; not just sketched) for *My Antonia*.

4. Have students write a plot summary of a book called *The Cuzaks* in which the story of Antonia's children is told. Using the information given about the different children, students should project what will happen to each of them in their own lives. Consider that Jim Burden or many of the other characters in Antonia's life may be an influence on the children.

5. Have students write samples of what letters may have been written and sent to and from Antonia and Jim over the 20 years following the end of the novel.

6. Hold a class discussion in which students compare and contrast life in the pioneer days with life in America today. Consider the impact of our pioneering heritage on our attitudes and lifestyles today.

7. Compare and contrast *My Antonia* with other books students may have read about pioneers and pioneer life, such as the *Little House* books by Laura Ingalls Wilder.

8. Discuss different kinds of pioneers and frontiers. Starting back with early civilizations and going through present-day frontiers. Consider also, other types of frontiers rather than physical land frontiers, frontiers of exploration in the areas of science and technology.

WORD SEARCH - *My Antonia*

All words in this list are associated with *My Antonia*. The words are placed backwards, forward, diagonally, up and down. The included words are listed below the word searches.

```
J A J W P F D H K Q J R P S Z G B Z Z D B C B T
L L M W L A L P C J J L D B N J M L L F A X S H
C N Q B N Y V P T L D E A B V A S Y I T R X C V
K L R C R H W E A I R R T B Y K L H N A B A W
V P E R T O J E L I N E K P R A Y E R S D N A L
M S A R C Y S Y H A N Y D D I K R R F R N Y E Y
S M A K I F W C V B W O N I S C R W A I P Y R L
X I N P M C M O H R R U T N C N N Z S C L R T N
N H A R L I N G S A A A I N S I Z I E J S M S Z
F E G H J O P Y H L K D L H A I U I C E A N K T
P K B P D S U T F L R M C L L K R S S R E K F R
C G Y R H W R G U O K U V B O I G A E V O N E B
Y U W G A A B Y H E F R D O A C E K A L E T G F
V J Z P M S Q W I S F V B R R S S E H D T N T Q
W X V A C G K J T B X J P R I S T T R U X G Q O
W P D W K L A A W J G F G D C S P U C H H T V P
N M D K C R C F G W N S P B K K B S P K R J S C
R F S L K Z Q T M C T P L G T W J M V W T Q J W
K N H M R M Z T C G B R M K G J N L M B V C S G
T Z V C J F W F W D N L B D N K B H Y Z G B H C
```

AMBROSCH	CUZAK	LAUNDRY	PRAIRIE
ANTONIA	DANCES	LENA	PRAYERS
BARN	DISEASES	LIFE	SNAKE
BLIND	DONOVAN	MAREK	STEAVENS
BLIZZARD	FUCHS	MARRY	SUICIDE
BOOK	HARLINGS	MARTHA	TINY
BURDEN	HIRED	NEBRASKA	TRAIN
CATHER	JAKE	ORDINSKY	VANNIS
CLERIC	JELINEK	OTTO	YULKA
COLLAR	JIM	PAVEL	
COW	KRAJIEK	PICNIC	
CUTTER	LAND	PLOUGH	

CROSSWORD - *My Antonia*

137

CROSSWORD CLUES - *My Antonia*

ACROSS

4. Greedy usurer, employs Antonia
5. Reason Jake can't go Christmas shopping in town
7. Jim made a cloth-covered --- for Antonia and Yulka
10. Every one
11. We learn more about the hired girls as Jim talks and listens to them at the ---
13. Otto's last name
14. Makes Mr. Shimerda's coffin
15. Dressmaker who does not marry
16. Jim hit it with a spade and killed it
17. The Shimerdas were in --- circumstances in the winter; urgent; desperate
19. Jim's advisor and teacher
20. Hits Ambrosch, causing a little feud
22. Antonia's little sister
23. She was a rich mine of ---, like the founders of early races.
24. Present singular of 'to be'
25. Gets rich by a gold claim
27. Antonia's first baby
29. The scene with the rattlesnake was symbolic of the garden of --
30. Sick
31. Marries Antonia
33. Time when the sun first comes up
34. Place where Mr. Shimerda's body was found
39. Close to
40. Bohemian Peter who takes advantage of Shimerdas
42. Definite article
44. Lena's neighbor
46. Bring dance to Black Hawk
48. We go to Black Hawk, -----.
53. Employ Antonia; Jim's neighbors
54. Antonia's brother
56. Myself
57. Attempt

DOWN

1. Narrator
2. Antonia quit working for the Harlings rather than give up these
3. Deserts Antonia
4. The feud between the Burdens and Shimerdas was over a horse ---
5. --- d'Arnault; piano player
6. Jake thinks you're 'likely to get --- from foreigners.'
7. Jim's last name
8. The Danish --- girls
9. Jim went to see this widow to find out about Antonia and Larry Donovan
11. He threw the bride and groom to the wolves
12. Peace offering from Burdens to Shimerdas
18. --- girls; daughters of immigrant farmers who came to town to work
19. Author
20. Anton who helped the Shimerdas after Mr. S's death
21. Mr. Shimerda -----ed himself
23. 'There was nothing but ---; ... the material out of which countries are made.'
25. Place Jim first heard of Antonia
26. Because Mr. S committed ---, he couldn't be buried in the Norwegian or Catholic cemeteries
27. Shimerdas' mentally retarded son
28. Steal from someone
32. Lena was determined not to --- because she liked her freedom
35. Jim's life-long friend
36. Things people must have (as opposed to 'wants')
37. Everyone at the Burden farm attends evening --- to bring the day to a close
38. The 'great black figure' that suddenly appeared on the face of the sun'
41. Stops; comes to a halt or a close
43. They put Mr. S's coffin into a --- where there might later be roads
45. Antonia's build; very thin
47. Coordinating conjunction
49. Indefinite article
50. People thought Lena was a --- (a promiscuous woman)
51. Inquire; Jim went to the widow to --- about Antonia
52. Shed tears
55. Personal pronoun for Jim (or any male)

CROSSWORD ANSWER KEY - *My Antonia*

MATCHING/QUIZ WORKSHEET 1 - *My Antonia*

____ 1. SNAKE	A. Everyone at the Burden farm attends evening --- to bring the day to a close

____ 2. LENA	B. Jim made a cloth-covered --- for Antonia and Yulka

____ 3. BLIZZARD	C. Reason Jake can't go Christmas shopping in town

____ 4. TRAIN	D. The Danish --- girls

____ 5. ORDINSKY	E. Peace offering from Burdens to Shimerdas

____ 6. PICNIC	F. Jim's advisor and teacher

____ 7. COW	G. Jim hit it with a spade and killed it

____ 8. CUTTER	H. Lena's neighbor

____ 9. PRAYERS	I. Dressmaker who does not marry

____ 10. CUZAK	J. Place Jim first heard of Antonia

____ 11. VANNIS	K. He threw the bride and groom to the wolves

____ 12. LAUNDRY	L. We learn more about the hired girls as Jim talks and listens to them at the ---

____ 13. OTTO	M. Bring dance to Black Hawk

____ 14. NEBRASKA	N. --- girls; daughters of immigrant farmers who came to town to work

____ 15. PAVEL	O. Makes Mr. Shimerda's coffin

____ 16. DONOVAN	P. Greedy usurer, employs Antonia

____ 17. BOOK	Q. Deserts Antonia

____ 18. HIRED	R. We go to Black Hawk, -----.

____ 19. CLERIC	S. Marries Antonia

____ 20. STEAVENS	T. Jim went to see this widow to find out about Antonia and Larry Donovan

MATCHING/QUIZ WORKSHEET 2 - *My Antonia*

____ 1. TINY	A. 'There was nothing but ---; ... the material out of which countries are made.'
____ 2. BLIND	B. The feud between the Burdens and Shimerdas was over a horse ---
____ 3. COLLAR	C. Because Mr. S committed ---, he couldn't be buried in the Norwegian or Catholic cemeteries
____ 4. JIM	D. Hits Ambrosch, causing a little feud
____ 5. HARLINGS	E. He threw the bride and groom to the wolves
____ 6. LAND	F. Anton who helped the Shimerdas after Mr. S's death
____ 7. PRAIRIE	G. Peace offering from Burdens to Shimerdas
____ 8. CUTTER	H. Jim's last name
____ 9. PICNIC	I. Jim made a cloth-covered --- for Antonia and Yulka
____ 10. LIFE	J. She was a rich mine of ---, like the founders of early races.
____ 11. COW	K. --- girls; daughters of immigrant farmers Who came to town to work
____ 12. JELINEK	L. Ambrosch asks if --- dogs are good to eat
____ 13. SUICIDE	M. Narrator
____ 14. BOOK	N. Employ Antonia; Jim's neighbors
____ 15. PAVEL	O. Antonia's first baby
____ 16. HIRED	P. Greedy usurer, employs Antonia
____ 17. MARTHA	Q. Place where Mr. Shimerda's body was found
____ 18. JAKE	R. --- d'Arnault; piano player
____ 19. BARN	S. Gets rich by a gold claim
____ 20. BURDEN	T. We learn more about the hired girls as Jim talks and listens to them at the —

KEY: MATCHING/QUIZ WORKSHEETS - *My Antonia*

Worksheet 1	Worksheet 2
1. G	1. S
2. I	2. R
3. C	3. B
4. J	4. M
5. H	5. N
6. L	6. A
7. E	7. L
8. P	8. P
9. A	9. T
10. S	10. J
11. M	11. G
12. D	12. F
13. O	13. C
14. R	14. I
15. K	15. E
16. Q	16. K
17. B	17. O
18. N	18. D
19. F	19. Q
20. T	20. H

JUGGLE LETTER REVIEW GAME CLUE SHEET - *My Antonia*

SCRAMBLED	WORD	CLUE
KAJE	JAKE	Hits Ambrosch, causing a little feud
TURTEC	CUTTER	Greedy usurer, employs Antonia
ONANITA	ANTONIA	Jim's life-long friend
NANSIV	VANNIS	Bring dance to Black Hawk
LANSHRIG	HARLINGS	Employ Antonia; Jim's neighbors
RELICC	CLERIC	Jim's advisor and teacher
MIJ	JIM	Narrator
RAMHAT	MARTHA	Antonia's first baby
CBOSAMRH	AMBROSCH	Antonia's brother
NEAL	LENA	Dressmaker who does not marry
TOOT	OTTO	Makes Mr. Shimerda's coffin
NANVOOD	DONOVAN	Deserts Antonia
ZUACK	CUZAK	Marries Antonia
SIROYNKD	ORDINSKY	Lena's neighbor
NYTI	TINY	Gets rich by a gold claim
HATREC	CATHER	Author
VALEP	PAVEL	He threw the bride and groom to the wolves
KEANS	SNAKE	Jim hit it with a spade and killed it
RATIN	TRAIN	Place Jim first heard of Antonia
REDBUN	BURDEN	Jim's last name
BASKANER	NEBRASKA	We go to Black Hawk, -----.
ASIDESSE	DISEASES	Jake thinks you're 'likely to get --- from foreigners.'
SHCFU	FUCHS	Otto's last name
DANL	LAND	There was nothing but ---; ... the material out of which countries are made.'
RAPYERS	PRAYERS	Everyone at the Burden farm attends evening --- to bring the day to a close
KJRAEIK	KRAJIEK	Bohemian Peter who takes advantage of Shimerdas
KALUY	YULKA	Antonia's little sister
EPAIRIR	PRAIRIE	Ambrosch asks if --- dogs are good to eat
KEMAR	MAREK	Shimerdas' mentally handicapped son

Antonia Juggle Letter Review Clues Continued

ZIBLAZRD	BLIZZARD	Reason Jake can't go Christmas shopping in town
KOBO	BOOK	Jim made a cloth-covered --- for Antonia and Yulka
NARB	BARN	Place where Mr. Shimerda's body was found
JINEKEL	JELINEK	Anton who helped the Shimerdas after Mr. S's death
DUISICE	SUICIDE	Because Mr. S committed ---, he couldn't be buried in the Norwegian or Catholic cemeteries
ROLCAL	COLLAR	The feud between the Burdens and Shimerdas was over a horse ---
OWC	COW	Peace offering from Burdens to Shimerdas
DINBL	BLIND	--- d'Arnault; piano player
DREIH	HIRED	--- girls; daughters of immigrant farmers who came to town to work
RAYLUND	LAUNDRY	The Danish --- girls
SANDCE	DANCES	Antonia quit working for the Harlings rather than give up these
NICCIP	PICNIC	We learn more about the hired girls as Jim talks and listens to them at the ---
GLOUPH	PLOUGH	The 'great black figure' that 'suddenly appeared on the face of the sun'
RAMRY	MARRY	Lena was determined not to --- because she liked her freedom
VEATSENS	STEAVENS	Jim went to see this widow to find out about Antonia and Larry Donovan
FIEL	LIFE	She was a rich mine of ---, like the founders of early races.

VOCABULARY RESOURCE MATERIALS

VOCABULARY WORD SEARCH My Antonia

```
T A C I T U R N R E P R O A C H V
L I M P I D V S P H E A P T C N T
T J O V I A L I T Y T D R O Y D Y
A R B L A M E N T A U L D R D B D
C E E J U D I C I A L R E P O S E
Q M W S V H D V Q R A W Y O L Y C
U I I P I Q U A N T N F A R V B O
I S L M N T P M V V T R C R I L R
T S D A D R A Y B Z L E O O T U U
G H E X I E O W X L Y S V R A S M
F X R I C U S R I M E H E A L T Y
S O E M T H S P A N B E T T I E R
U G D S I F I U E C D T I I T R E
P E L D V Y U L R R U I N O Y E T
I L I G E L B R L Y A L G N D D I
N D V Y H R Z Q T O L D A N J S C
E I E C O V E R T I C F O R A H E
D N R S A T I E T Y V K S C F N N
Q G Y M A L A D Y F H E S G C T T
```

ACQUIT	HILLOCKS	PIQUANT
ARROYO	HUMBLE	REMISS
BEWILDERED	INDIGNANT	REPOSE
BLUSTERED	JOVIALITY	REPROACH
COVERT	JUDICIAL	RETICENT
COVETING	LAMENT	SATIETY
DECORUM	LIMPID	STALWART
DESPERADO	LIVERY	SUPINE
DRAY	MALADY	TACITURN
FODDER	MAXIMS	TORPOR
FRESHET	ORACULAR	USURY
FURTIVE	ORATION	VINDICTIVE
GELDING	PETULANTLY	VITALITY

VOCABULARY WORD SEARCH My Antonia

```
T  A  C  I  T  U  R  N  R  E     P  R  O  A  C  H
L  I  M  P  I  D        S        E     A     T
   J  O  V  I  A  L  I  T  Y  T        R  O
A  R  B  L  A  M  E  N  T  A  U        R           D
C  E  E  J  U  D  I  C  I  A  L  R  E  P  O  S  E
Q  M  W     V  H                 A  W     O     Y  C
U  I  P  I  Q  U  A  N  T     N  F  A  R  V     B  O
I  S  L  M  N        M        T  R  C  R  I     L  R
T  S  D  A  D  R  A  Y  B     L  E  O  O  T     U  U
      E  X  I  E  O        L  Y  S     V  R  A  S  M
   F  R  I  C  U  S  R  I     E  H  E  A  L     T
   S  O  E  M  T  H  S  P  A  N     E  T  T  I     R
   U  G  D  S  I  F  I  U  E  C  D  T  I  I  T  R  E
   P  E  L  D  V     U  L  R  R  U  I  N  O  Y  E  T
   I  L  I     E        R  L  Y  A  L  G     N  D  I
   N  D  V        R           T  O     D  A  N     C
   E  I  E  C  O  V  E  R  T  I  C     O  R  A     E
      N  R  S  A  T  I  E  T  Y  V  K           N  N
      G  Y  M  A  L  A  D  Y        E  S           T
```

ACQUIT	HILLOCKS	PIQUANT
ARROYO	HUMBLE	REMISS
BEWILDERED	INDIGNANT	REPOSE
BLUSTERED	JOVIALITY	REPROACH
COVERT	JUDICIAL	RETICENT
COVETING	LAMENT	SATIETY
DECORUM	LIMPID	STALWART
DESPERADO	LIVERY	SUPINE
DRAY	MALADY	TACITURN
FODDER	MAXIMS	TORPOR
FRESHET	ORACULAR	USURY
FURTIVE	ORATION	VINDICTIVE
GELDING	PETULANTLY	VITALITY

VOCABULARY CROSSWORD - *My Antonia*

VOCABULARY CROSSWORD CLUES - *My Antonia*

ACROSS

4. Unceasingly; persistently; constantly
9. Moral corruption
11. Like a judge; pertaining to the administration of justice
12. Prefix meaning 'small'
14. Bestowing; giving
17. A heavy cart without sides
18. Bold or desperate outlaw
19. Mr. Shimerda and Mr. Burden, for example
20. A feeling or expression of grief or mourning
22. Inform
25. Not any
26. Lending money at an excessively high rate of interest
27. Zestful intensity of feeling
28. Alike
32. Immediately following; subsequent
33. Lying on one's back
34. Ingest food
35. Distinctive uniform
36. Spacious
42. Narrator
45. Allow
46. Dormant or inactive state
47. Bohemian Peter who takes advantage of Shimerdas
48. A single
49. Go on horseback
50. Freed from blame or accusation
51. Sudden overflow of a stream from heavy rain

DOWN

1. Confused; at a loss
2. Short statements of moral truths
3. In an ill-tempered manner
5. Unhappy
6. Appropriate conduct
7. Formal speech; pompous speech
8. 'There was nothing but ---; ... the material out of which countries are made.'
10. Scornful
13. Nobleness; forgivingness; graciousness
14. Want
15. Food for livestock
16. A castrated horse
17. Made smaller or less
21. Spoke noisily and boastfully
23. Peace offering from Burdens to Simerdas
24. Appease; make up
27. Creek that is sometimes dry or dry gulch
29. Small hills
30. Clear; calm
36. Not done openly; at least partially concealed
37. A disease or bad condition
38. Makes Mr. Shimerda's coffin
39. Sheaves of grain stacked upright to dry
40. Resting
41. Place where Mr. Shimerda's body was found
43. Hits Ambrosch, causing a little feud
44. Dressmaker who does not marry

VOCABULARY CROSSWORD ANSWER KEY - *My Antonia*

VOCABULARY WORKSHEET 1 - *My Antonia*

____ 1. Bestowing; giving
    A. Vitality   B. Conferring   C. Implored   D. Joviality

____ 2. Moral disapproval
    A. Deferred   B. Propitiatory   C. Disapprobation   D. Indolently

____ 3. Creek that is sometimes dry or dry gulch
    A. Arroyo   B. Forestalled   C. Covert   D. Reproach

____ 4. Lending money at an excessively high rate of interest
    A. Maxims   B. Furtive   C. Usury   D. Joviality

____ 5. Food for livestock
    A. Fodder   B. Indulgently   C. Remissness   D. Inveterate

____ 6. A castrated horse
    A. Freshet   B. Licentiousness   C. Gelding   D. Supine

____ 7. Wiped out; annihilated
    A. Obliterated   B. Slavishly   C. Vindictive   D. Petulantly

____ 8. Alteration in the pitch of the voice
    A. Inflection   B. Encumbered   C. Propitiate   D. Coveting

____ 9. Anxiously; uneasily
    A. Apprehensively   B. Torpor   C. Furtive   D. Gelding

____ 10. Pathetically
    A. Parsimonious   B. Taciturn   C. Reticent   D. Piteously

____ 11. Sudden overflow of a stream from heavy rain
    A. Blustered   B. Gesticulations   C. Torpor   D. Freshet

____ 12. Term used to characterize a person or a thing
    A. Ensuing   B. Apprehensively   C. Epithet   D. Humble

____ 13. Retreat
    A. Inflection   B. Hermitage   C. Vermillion   D. Supine

____ 14. Wise; prophetic; sacred
    A. Oracular   B. Credulousness   C. Boisterously   D. Blustered

____ 15. Frugal; stingy
    A. Contemptuous   B. Assiduously   C. Parsimonious   D. Indignant

____ 16. Strolled
    A. Joviality   B. Disapprobation   C. Sauntered   D. Fastidious

____ 17. Revengeful
    A. Vermillion   B. Vindictive   C. Obliterated   D. Fastidious

____ 18. Submitted to; gave in to
    A. Inflection   B. Vermillion   C. Reticent   D. Deferred

____ 19. Effort; action; activity
    A. Piteously   B. Inveterate   C. Constitution   D. Exertion

____ 20. Without resistance; without opposition
    A. Repose   B. Resistless   C. Parsimonious   D. Decorum

VOCABULARY WORKSHEET 2 - *My Antonia*

____ 1. INDOLENCE   A. Laziness

____ 2. LUMINARIES   B. Showing a willingness to take on new projects

____ 3. PIQUANT   C. State of exhaustion or inactivity

____ 4. VINDICTIVE   D. Appease; make up

____ 5. STALWART   E. Food for livestock

____ 6. ARDOUR   F. Something that gives off light

____ 7. FODDER   G. Sorrowfully; in a melancholy way

____ 8. PROPITIATE   H. Charming; interesting; attraction

____ 9. ENTERPRISING   I. Strong; stout

____ 10. BOISTEROUSLY   J. Extremely; beyond normal bounds

____ 11. PLAINTIVELY   K. Moral corruption

____ 12. USURY   L. About to die or become obsolete

____ 13. INDIFFERENCE   M. Zestful intensity of feeling

____ 14. MORIBUND   N. Dormant or inactive state

____ 15. IMMODERATELY   O. Loudly and lacking restraint

____ 16. ENSUING   P. Revengeful

____ 17. TACITURN   Q. Immediately following; subsequent

____ 18. DEBAUCHERY   R. Lending money at an excessively high rate of interest

____ 19. TORPOR   S. Lack of care or concern

____ 20. LASSITUDE   T. Doesn't talk much

KEY: VOCABULARY WORKSHEETS - *My Antonia*

Worksheet 1	Worksheet 2
1. B	1. A
2. C	2. F
3. A	3. H
4. C	4. P
5. A	5. I
6. C	6. M
7. A	7. E
8. A	8. D
9. A	9. B
10. D	10. O
11. D	11. G
12. C	12. R
13. B	13. S
14. A	14. L
15. C	15. J
16. C	16. Q
17. B	17. T
18. D	18. K
19. D	19. N
20. B	20. C

VOCABULARY JUGGLE LETTER REVIEW GAME CLUES - *My Antonia*

SCRAMBLED	WORD	CLUE
UACTIQ	ACQUIT	Freed from blame or accusation
PEHAPSVLIYEENR	APPREHENSIVELY	Anxiously; uneasily
DUAROR	ARDOUR	Zestful intensity of feeling
ROYRAO	ARROYO	Creek that is sometimes dry or dry gulch
SSYDUUAISOL	ASSIDUOUSLY	Unceasingly; persistently; constantly
EEDDERWILB	BEWILDERED	Confused; at a loss
SREBULDTE	BLUSTERED	Spoke noisily and boastfully
EOISLSYORBUT	BOISTEROUSLY	Loudly and lacking restraint
MUDCOOMSOI	COMMODIOUS	Spacious
FONGRERCNI	CONFERRING	Bestowing; giving
STTIOCNOUNTI	CONSTITUTION	Physical makeup of a person
RSONDNEATCI	CONSTRAINED	Restrained; held back
MNOESOTUUCTP	CONTEMPTUOUS	Scornful
GEOTINVC	COVETING	Wanting
ROTVEC	COVERT	Not done openly; at least partially concealed
EULNSSEOSDRUC	CREDULOUSNESS	Gullibility
BERYUCDEAH	DEBAUCHERY	Moral corruption
CMODURE	DECORUM	Appropriate conduct
EERERDFD	DEFERRED	Submitted to; gave in to
AEPDODRES	DESPERADO	Bold or desperate outlaw
ELOIDEDPS	DESPOILED	Plundered; robbed
MEDIDISIHN	DIMINISHED	Made smaller or less
NPIDBIOROASPAT	DISAPPROBATION	Moral disapproval
RAYD	DRAY	A heavy cart without sides
CENDEBUREM	ENCUMBERED	Hindered; weighed down
EIUSGNN	ENSUING	Immediately following; subsequent
GRISTERENPIN	ENTERPRISING	Showing a willingness to take on new projects
PETETHI	EPITHET	Term used to characterize a person or a thing
XOTERENI	EXERTION	Effort; action; activity
STOUFSADII	FASTIDIOUS	Particular
DREFOD	FODDER	Food for livestock
TELFESROLDA	FORESTALLED	Delayed
STERHFE	FRESHET	Sudden overflow of a stream from heavy rain
VUTEFRI	FURTIVE	Shifty; stealthy
GIGLDNE	GELDING	A castrated horse
CSAGUONTELISIT	GESTICULATIONS	Vigorous gestures; body movements used for emphasis in speech

MHERAGETI	HERMITAGE	Retreat
OHSILKCL	HILLOCKS	Small hills
EUMHLB	HUMBLE	Knock down a peg or two; give a lower station or condition to
TMIOYLMAEDER	IMMODERATELY	Extremely; beyond normal bounds
RDILMOEP	IMPLORED	Begged; asked earnestly
FENCIDREEFIN	INDIFFERENCE	Lack of care or concern
NIDNATNIG	INDIGNANT	Angered by an unjust condition
ONEELCIND	INDOLENCE	Laziness
YONDNLELIT	INDOLENTLY	Lazily
GINYNUDLLTE	INDULGENTLY	Leniently
TIFMRNYII	INFIRMITY	Frailty; feebleness; weakness
OENINFTILC	INFLECTION	Alteration in the pitch of the voice
GISNANTYLUNII	INSINUATINGLY	Suggestively; ingratiatingly
TESRSCIERNO	INTERCESSOR	One who is a mediator on someone else's behalf
EINTRETVAE	INVETERATE	Habitual; deep-rooted
JLYOVTIIA	JOVIALITY	Hearty good cheer
IIULADJC	JUDICIAL	Like a judge; pertaining to the administration of justice
MANETL	LAMENT	A feeling or expression of grief or mourning
USATLIDSE	LASSITUDE	State of exhaustion or inactivity
SENLCUISOSENIT	LICENTIOUSNESS	Having no regard for accepted rules
PILDMI	LIMPID	Clear; calm
RELIVY	LIVERY	Distinctive uniform
RULINSEMAI	LUMINARIES	Something that gives off light
MAMGANYINTI	MAGNANIMITY	Nobleness; forgivingness; graciousness
ALYDAM	MALADY	A disease or bad condition
SAXIMM	MAXIMS	Short statements of moral truths
ORESOITUIMR	MERITORIOUS	Deserving praise or reward
UNBORDMI	MORIBUND	About to die or become obsolete
BLADOTETERI	OBLITERATED	Wiped out; annihilated
SEVPOPSERI	OPPRESSIVE	Difficult to bear; harsh
LACRARUO	ORACULAR	Wise; prophetic; sacred
NOORTAI	ORATION	Formal speech; pompous speech
INPOSRASUMOI	PARSIMONIOUS	Frugal; stingy
UNREOYRCTPF	PERFUNCTORY	Doing something with little interest or care
NUTLLYATPE	PETULANTLY	In an ill-tempered manner
QUATNIP	PIQUANT	Charming; interesting; attraction
IOSYTEPUL	PITEOUSLY	Pathetically
VALTIIPNYEL	PLAINTIVELY	Sorrowfully; in a melancholy way
ETAITIPORP	PROPITIATE	Appease; make up

POORTIAPRITY	PROPITIATORY	Conciliatory; appeasing
SIRESENMSS	REMISSNESS	Negligence
TREUNACNIYOR	RENUNCIATORY	Giving up; sending away
SOREEP	REPOSE	Resting
PREHOCAR	REPROACH	An expression of criticism, disappointment, or blame
LISSSSTERE	RESISTLESS	Without resistance; without opposition
NTTIRCEE	RETICENT	Reserved
EATYITS	SATIETY	The condition of being over-full or over-satisfied
NDEERAUST	SAUNTERED	Strolled
KOSSCH	SHOCKS	Sheaves of grain stacked upright to dry
HALSLYVSI	SLAVISHLY	Like a slave
CIOSTOULSI	SOLICITOUS	Attentive; careful; meticulous
WALTRATS	STALWART	Strong; stout
PURTIRS	STIRRUP	Flat-based metal loop used to support a horse rider's foot
RUSILICSEPUO	SUPERCILIOUS	Haughty; disdainful
UNPISE	SUPINE	Lying on one's back
NUTTARCI	TACITURN	Doesn't talk much
ROPROT	TORPOR	Dormant or inactive state
LOMDFIEUNLI	UNMOLLIFIED	Not calmed in temper or feeling
CULSOURNUSPU	UNSCRUPULOUS	Without morals; without a personal obligation to do right
YURUS	USURY	Lending money at an excessively high rate of interest
LERVILOMNI	VERMILLION	Bright reddish-orange color
LUTIVCAS	VICTUALS	Food for people
DETICINVIV	VINDICTIVE	Revengeful
TALIYTIV	VITALITY	Vigor; energy

www.ingramcontent.com/pod-product-compliance
Lightning Source LLC
Chambersburg PA
CBHW051410070526
44584CB00023B/3365